To my loving
sister Barbara
God's blessings
on you and His guidance
in your life.
Your sister, Pat
May 4, 2016

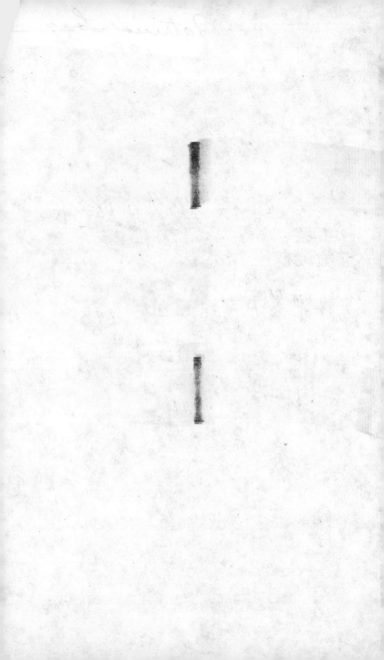

BERNADETTE
The Only Witness

BERNADETTE
The Only Witness

by

Rev. John W. Lynch, S.M.

ST. PAUL EDITIONS

IMPRIMI POTEST:
 Very Reverend Albert DiIanni, S.M.
 Provincial of the Northeast U.S.A.
 Province of the Society of Mary

NIHIL OBSTAT:
 Rev. Msgr. Matthew P. Stapleton

IMPRIMATUR:
 + Humberto Cardinal Medeiros
 Archbishop of Boston

Library of Congress Cataloging in Publication Data

Lynch, John W.
 Bernadette—the only witness.

 1. Bernadette, Saint, 1844-1879. 2. Christian
saints—France—Lourdes—Biography. 3. Lourdes (France)
—Biography. I. Title.
BX4700.S65L9   282'.092'4   [B]   81-1725
                                                       AACR2

ISBN 0-8198-1104-1 cloth
     0-8198-1105-X paper

Printed in the U.S.A. by the Daughters of St. Paul
50 St. Paul's Ave., Boston, Ma. 02130

The Daughters of St. Paul are an international congregation
of religious women serving the Church with the communi-
cations media.

CONTENTS

Prologue

Learning to cope is everyone's business. Bernadette, without ever intending it, teaches people how she succeeded—not without setbacks—in making do with the little she had; and in making her many aches and pains work to her profit.

Her story is most fascinating. The more one gets to know her, the more lovable she becomes. She broke into the limelight in an altogether stunning way, and after being exposed to the glare of publicity she was never again to capture the anonymity she so passionately craved.

This story could never have been told without the help of the exhaustive research of L'Abbé René Laurentin, whose scholarly works (untranslated as yet) *Logia de Bernadette* (3 Vols.); *Bernadette Vous Parle* (2 Vols.); and *Le Visage de Bernadette* (2 Vols.) were indispensable. Indebtedness is also due to Rev. André Ravier, S.J., whose *Le Corps de Bernadette* produced the details contained in the Epilogue.

Bernadette

It's a bit of a wonder that Bernadette ever came to be. Her mother's father, Augustin Castérot, called Justin, began the whole process by dying in a wagon accident on the Pouyferré road in 1841. His death left the Boly Mill to his widow, Claire, who was also left with three young daughters and an eleven-year-old son. She needed a man to operate the mill and decided to remedy the situation by marrying off her eldest daughter, the nineteen-year-old Bernarde; her new son-in-law would take over operations. Her choice was François Soubirous, a thirty-four-year-old unmarried miller. She approached him with the proposition, but though he went along with the marriage idea, he balked at the choice of Bernarde. His preference was the seventeen-year-old Louise, with the dark-brown hair and the blue eyes. Bypassing her eldest did not suit the widow at all, nor the rejected Bernarde either, but there was nothing she could do to change Francois' mind. Louise and Francois were married January 9, 1843, and one year later, January 7, 1844, Louise had a baby girl.

The baby girl, baptized two days later, cried during most of the ceremony, much to the disgust of her godfather, her fourteen-year-old cousin, Jean-Marie Védère. Her godmother, Aunt Bernarde, the girl her father had rejected, was none too pleased either, since the baptizing priest inverted her godchild's names. The day before at the town hall, the baby girl had been registered Bernarde-Marie; now at the baptism the priest baptized her Marie-Bernarde. Aunt Bernarde was to get over her pique, because for the rest of her life Aunt Bernarde's godchild was to be called Bernadette by almost everyone.

When God chooses people for special tasks, He has a way of confounding everyone, including the chosen one. In the case of Bernadette, He acted in His usual, bewildering way. His preparations had the appearance of a pile of jigsaw pieces, cut and shaped every which way; but when these pieces fell in place, who could do anything but admire the result?

Bernadette's godfather's prediction that she would be nothing but a cry-baby proved false, because she turned out to be a lovable, smiling baby, whom her maiden aunts tended to spoil. They did not have much of a chance, however, since her mother's bodice accidentally caught fire, causing her enough injury to prevent her from nursing her child. Aunt Bernarde found a woman who had just lost her baby son and who agreed to nurse Bernadette for five francs a month, payable in cash or wheat. Marie Laguës, the newly-found nurse, lived in Bartrès, three miles from Lourdes, where Bernadette stayed until her mother wanted her back home after the death of Bernadette's baby brother, Jean-Marie, only two months old. Bernadette was to have six brothers and two sisters, but only one sister, Marie, called Toinette, and two brothers, a second Jean-Marie and Bernard-Pierre were to live beyond the age of ten. Justin died at ten; the four others died in infancy.

In Bernadette's childhood, her family enjoyed relative comfort at the Boly Mill, her birthplace; but this was to be of temporary nature. Her father, François, ran the mill and from his earnings had to support his mother-in-law's family as well as his own. Of an easy-going disposition, he let debts owed him go uncollected, and always insisted that his customers be served cheese and wine on their calls, a kindness that ate up his profits. His wife, Louise, could see no fault in him and went along with his unbusinesslike ways. When he could no longer pay his own bills and let the mill go into disrepair, his customers began trading elsewhere. Over and above this, the title to the Boly Mill had never been quite clear, and when the rightful owner decided to run it himself, François had to find himself another location. He failed at every location he tried, until he could not afford to pay rent anywhere and was forced to accept a dark, dank, room, formerly a jail, now owned by a cousin. This *Cachot*, as it was called, in the Rue des Petits Fossés, had to do as a home. To support his family, François had to do odd jobs; and Louise, his wife, had to do washing or had to work in the fields to help make ends meet. Bernadette had to stay home and tend the younger children: the reason she rarely went to school. The Soubirous had sunk to poverty level.

As a child Bernadette had been healthy enough, but at six she began to have asthma attacks, which were to plague her for the rest of her life. When she was eleven, a cholera epidemic struck the Lourdes area, making her one of its victims; but she somehow recovered from that. Any opportunity that could ease the burden at the *Cachot* was grasped, so that when Aunt Bernarde, who had by now married a cabaret-owner, had Bernadette stay with her for periods of time, her father did not mind having one less mouth to feed at home. The fare at Aunt Bernarde's was much better than at the *Cachot,* but Aunt Bernarde did not want a star boarder; Bernadette had to earn her keep. It's perhaps her cabaret experience that prompted Bernadette, years later, to advise Sister Vincent Garros, a very good friend of hers, who had been given an assignment to nurse in a hospital, to keep the door open whenever she had to tend men.

Because of her docility, Bernadette was not only a favorite with her godmother, Aunt Bernarde, but was also a pet of her foster mother, Marie Laguës, who never forgot the baby she had nursed. When Bernadette was thirteen, Marie Laguës asked to have her come to Bartrès to help her. Bernadette's mother agreed to let her go, provided she was able to attend the catechism classes in Bartrès, preparatory to making her First Communion. Once there, Bernadette rarely went to the classes, if at all, because as

soon as she arrived she was given the Laguës'
sheep to tend. Being a shepherdess left little
time for catechism classes. Marie Lagues tried
teaching Bernadette herself, but that proved fu-
tile. Bernadette could not keep anything in her
head, because all she knew was the dialect of
the region and all the books were in French. As
a teacher, Marie Laguës had very little patience,
which did not help the situation. After six or
seven months of tending sheep, Bernadette sent
messages to her parents to bring her home so
that she could go to the catechism classes in
Lourdes to prepare for her First Communion
there. Since she wanted this so badly, her parents finally brought her back to Lourdes at
the end of January, 1858. Bernadette had just
turned fourteen.

Massabielle

February 11, 1858, arrived cold and dreary. The Soubirous were short of firewood, and Bernadette offered to go in search of some, but her mother thought the cold weather would do nothing but aggravate Bernadette's asthma. She relented, however, when Jeanne Abadie, nicknamed "Baloum," dropped in and said she would go with the Soubirous girls. Bernadette, Toinette, and "Baloum" started out and worked their way towards a dismal part of Lourdes, called *Massabielle*. They arrived at a chilly stream, across which the two younger girls threw their sabots, and screamingly ran through the spine-tingling water. Bernadette, who had to wear stockings because of her asthma, did not want to be left alone. She tried to find stones to throw in the water, on which she could hop without getting her feet wet, but she could not. She then asked "Baloum" to carry her across, because "Baloum" was strongly built; but she refused, adding a mild oath to punctuate her refusal. Bernadette rebuked her for the use of the oath, at which "Baloum" and Toinette ran off. Wanting to follow them, Bernadette resignedly began to remove her sabots and stockings. She had just begun when she heard a rush of

wind, but on looking around she could see nothing stirring. She continued doing what she
started and again heard the same sound of
rushing wind, this time in front of her. When
she looked up, she saw a bunch of branches and
brambles below a grotto shaking back and
forth, and above the branches and brambles
stood the most beautiful lady she had ever seen.

The lady was about sixteen or seventeen,
dressed in a white veil and gown, with a blue
sash at her waist. On her right arm she carried a
large rosary of white beads on a golden chain,
and on each bare foot was a yellow rose. Bernadette rubbed her eyes and looked again, but the
apparition was still there. Bewildered, she auto-
matically reached in her pocket for her rosary
beads and tried to make the sign of the cross to
begin the beads, but her hand fell back at her
side; only after the lady had signed herself was
Bernadette able to do the same. While Bernadette said her beads, the lady let her own beads
slip through her fingers, her lips motionless.
After the beads were over, the lady beckoned
Bernadette to come closer, but Bernadette did
not dare approach, at which the lady disappeared.

When Toinette and "Baloum" returned to
find Bernadette kneeling and praying, they
were indignant that she had not even gathered
one stick of wood, and voiced their anger. Bernadette, still bemused by what had happened,
asked them if they had seen anything out of the
ordinary. "No," they answered, "Did you?"
"Oh, then, I didn't either," she said. They be-

gan to walk home, but the unusual sight bothered Bernadette too much for her to drop the
subject. Her sister Toinette, now fully suspi-
cious, wheedled the information out of Bernadette, after she had promised not to tell anyone.
After Bernadette told her, Toinette was bursting
to tell what she had heard. When she got the
chance at home, she told her mother what Bernadette had told her. Louise Soubirous had
enough worries without adding this foolishness
to her load. She closely questioned Bernadette
and came to the conclusion that it was all in
Bernadette's imagination—she thought she saw
something that wasn't there. Though Bernadette insisted that she saw what she saw, her
mother disagreed and ended by forbidding Bernadette to go back to the grotto.

In the afternoon, Bernadette told "Baloum"
what had happened to her at Massabielle. It
didn't take long for all the neighbors to learn of
Bernadette's "so-called" vision.

During the usual family night prayers, Bernadette burst into tears, causing her mother
more worry. She consulted Aunt Romaine, who
lived upstairs, and her conclusion was the same:
the whole thing was an illusion.

The next day, Friday, Bernadette's thoughts
were filled with what had happened at the grotto, and she could not help saying, "Something
is pushing me to go to Massabielle." Her mother
had enough of this. "Get to work!" she exploded.

On Saturday, Bernadette went to confession and told the Abbé Pomian about what she

had seen at the grotto, but since he was only the chaplain at the Hospice of Lourdes he asked her permission to talk about this to the pastor of the parish, Dean Peyramale, to which she readily agreed. On being told, the pastor's answer was, "We'll have to wait."

The Girls

Bernadette's girl-chums, their curiosity fully aroused, wanted to know more about what had gone on at the grotto. On Sunday, February 14, they pleaded with Bernadette's mother to let Bernadette go back with them. After some moments of indecision, she gave in, on condition that Bernadette's father agreed. He was working at Cazenave's Stable. Off ran the gaggle of girls to see him. His answer was a flat, "No!" His employer took the girls' part. "After all," he said, "a lady with a rosary, that isn't anything very bad...." Bernadette's father sheepishly went along.

No matter how beautiful this lady was, these girls were not going to take any chances with her. They would stop at the church to get some holy water, with which Bernadette could sprinkle her.

They arrived at the grotto, knelt, and began to say their beads. At the end of the first decade the lady appeared, but only to Bernadette; the rest could see nothing but the dreary grotto. The girls urged Bernadette to use the holy water. She approached and liberally sprinkled the lady, saying at the same time, "If you come from God, stay; but if not, go away!" All that got was a smile from the lady. Bernadette then knelt and, becoming ecstatic, continued to say her rosary. Her companions, seeing her so motionless, became frightened.

"Baloum," who had arrived late, was peeved that her friends had not waited for her. To pay them back, she pushed a large stone down the hill on which she was standing. It rolled toward the kneeling girls, who squealed and scampered; and though it came dangerously close to Bernadette, she remained as still as a statue. Because they could not budge her, her companions thought her dead. More scared now, they called for help, which arrived in the person of Antoine Nicolau, who operated a mill nearby. While he and his mother pulled and pushed Bernadette to their mill, she kept gazing raptly in the direction of the grotto. At the mill, she returned to her usual self. Her mother, who had been sent for, arrived, and, angered at what was happening, absolutely forbade Bernadette ever to go back to the grotto.

The Arrogant Widow

After the second apparition, many of the adults thought the reports of the children stuff and nonsense, foolish tales about the sickly Soubirous girl. One woman did not think the tales so foolish. Jeanne-Marie Milhet, a wealthy widow, learned the gossip from her dressmaker, Antoinette Peyret. The widow Milhet was not a bona fide upper-class person; she had arrived at her wealth by way of being a servant who, somehow, got to marry her employer. She was looked down upon by the "society" of Lourdes, and was pretty well disliked by the "commoners" as well, for the way she had climbed up in the world. The only explanation for her getting into the third apparition scene is that occasionally she hired Bernadette's mother to work for her— showing again how low the fortunes of the Soubirous had sunk.

Antoinette Peyret, the widow's dressmaker, was a good soul who tried to live up to her duties as a sodalist in the Children of Mary. She figured the apparition to be the ghost of Elisa Latapie, the recently deceased president of the Children of Mary, now returning to ask for prayers. Convincing her employer, the widow Milhet, of her belief, she had the widow pay Bernadette's mother a visit. In spite of Bernadette's mother's determination not to let Bernadette return to the grotto, the widow and her dressmaker wore down her resistance and got her to allow Bernadette to go back, with them as her escorts.

They left for the grotto early on February 18, taking paper, pen, and ink along to have the apparition write down what she wanted. On their arrival they began to say their beads. Almost immediately Bernadette murmured, "She is here!" but her escorts could see nothing of the apparition. The beads over, Antoinette gave Bernadette the paper, pen, and ink to present to the apparition. The three approached the rock on which the lady stood, but the lady made a sign for only Bernadette to approach. Alone, Bernadette presented the writing material to the lady, who laughed and spoke for the first time, "It is not necessary to write down what I have to say." (The lady spoke in the dialect of the region, the only language Bernadette knew.) The impatient widow prodded Bernadette to speak, but Bernadette, turning to her all surprised, answered, "But I did ask her, very loud!" Her escorts hadn't heard a word. "And her answer?" asked the widow. "The lady began to laugh," said Bernadette. Feeling rejected again the widow told Bernadette to ask the lady if her presence was disagreeable to her. Her dressmaker, not wishing to be left out, added, "Ask the lady if we can return." To this the lady answered Bernadette, "There is nothing to prevent it."

After the apparition, Bernadette rose and said to Antoinette, "The lady looked at you a long time." The widow resented this attention to her dressmaker and her own exclusion, and petulantly said, "It was the candle she was looking at!" "No!" said Bernadette. "The lady looked and smiled." To express her displeasure, the widow warned, "If you are lying, God will punish you!"

On their way back, Bernadette revealed that the lady had further said: "Will you do me the favor of coming here for a fortnight?" After Bernadette's "Yes," the lady added, "I do not promise that you will be happy in this world, but in the next."

If the lady could not make Bernadette happy in this world, the widow could. At the *Cachot*, after Bernadette's mother gave her reluctant consent to her visits, the widow announced that she was going to take charge of Bernadette, and brought her to her home.

In the Lourdes region, the eldest daughter in the family enjoys the privilege of making decisions, and her word is law. Aunt Bernarde, the girl Bernadette's father had rejected in favor of her younger sister, Louise, was the eldest daughter and very much aware of her decision-making powers, not to mention that she was also Bernadette's godmother. Hearing of the widow Milhet's high-handed actions, Aunt Bernarde objected strenuously, and had Bernadette back in the *Cachot* after only two nights of the widow's hospitality. With this, the widow disappears from the story of Lourdes.

The Fortnight

In a town of four thousand, not much goes on that people are not aware of. Anything as outlandish as a girl having visions in such a forbidding place as Massabielle could not pass unnoticed by anyone. And what better topic of conversation! Not only that, but anyone who wanted to get into the act could do just that. The little girl-chums of Bernadette had wheedled Bernadette's parents' permission to allow her to go back to the grotto, and they were rewarded for their efforts by being present at the second apparition. The widow Milhet had plowed her way into the third apparition scene, taking her dressmaker along in her wake. Now, fifteen visits to the grotto were an open invitation for anyone who cared to, to become part of the happening.

One of the problems for chroniclers of those events in 1858 is that no one took notes of what occurred daily, so that when historians of the visions later began recording the facts many of the details had to be guessed at, not very satisfying to genuine historians. Bernadette herself cared little about dates or on what days various things happened; all she was happy about was that they were happening. Furthermore, even when she was not ecstatic during the visions, her whole attention was on the lady, not on what was going on around her. Some historians have tried to give a day-by-day report of what occurred, but their placing certain things on certain days is questionable. In spite of the difficulty in pinpointing items during the fortnight, the historians know what did happen.

Bernadette went daily to the grotto during those two weeks. The lady, on her part, appeared every day but two: Monday, February 22, and Friday, February 26. She appeared to no one except Bernadette. On the 19th, 20th, and 21st the lady appeared to Bernadette, and more and more people gathered at the grotto to see for themselves what was going on. It was this influx of people that bothered the authorities; had Bernadette been alone they would not have taken any notice.

As has been said, Bernadette had already told of her first vision to her confessor, the Abbé Pomian, who was the chaplain at the Hospice of Lourdes. Aware of all the talk in town, he did not want to get into this affair over his head. He asked her permission to speak to the pastor about what she had told him, to which she readily agreed. Meeting the pastor that evening on the road to Argelès, the Abbé Pomian told him of the matter. Much more keenly aware of the gossip, the pastor wisely answered, "We have to wait."

After the sixth vision on Sunday, February 21, some of the women told Bernadette that the Abbé Pene, the curate of the parish, wanted to see her. Trying to sidestep this visit, she said she did not know him. "He's a priest," the women told her. "You have to do what he says." She went and heard him tell her, "Now that this lady has promised you happiness in the next world, you can do as you like and not worry about your future." Her answer surprised him. "Oh!" she said smilingly, "that's not it at all. She'll make me happy only if I do good." Learning from her how she felt during her visions— "outside of this world and, afterwards, surprised to find myself right back in this world," the Abbé Pène was quite impressed with her. For some time the clergy were to follow a "hands off" policy.

It was the turn of the civil authorities to step in. After vespers that same Sunday, when Bernadette was coming out of church, someone tugged her by the arm and told her to follow him. He was a policeman, who took her around the corner of the church to the house of the Superintendent of Police. Dominique Jacomet was a middle-aged man, who had reached the top of his profession, very acutely aware of the reverential awe the townspeople had for him. Though feared, he was popular, having gained his popularity during the cholera epidemic of 1855, when, unlike what a good many of the other important people did, he remained at his post to take care of the sick and dying. The news of Bernadette's claims had reached Paris, where the state authorities, perturbed at the rumors from this sleepy little town that were making undesirable headlines, wanted this nonsense stopped. Through the chain of command, the orders had finally come down to the Superintendent of Police, Dominique Jacomet. He would scare Bernadette and forbid her to go to the grotto; then all those sheeplike crowds who followed her would quit going.

Bernadette had hedged on visiting Abbé Pène, because she did not know him. She was acquainted with Jacomet. Had he not arrested her father a year ago on the false charge of stealing flour from the baker for whom he was working? Rounding the corner of the town hall, Bernadette heard someone shout, "Poor Bernadette! They're going to put you in jail." "I'm not afraid," she answered. "If they put me in, they'll have to let me out!"

Once alone in Jacomet's house, she sat down she was bidden. The battle of wits to follow would appear to be no match between the self-confident Superintendent of Police and this puny, little, fourteen-year-old girl; but appearances are often deceiving. Most little girls would have frozen in such a presence, but Bernadette showed untapped reserves of courage.

"Are you the little girl who goes to Massabielle every day?"

"Yes, sir," she answered amiably.

"And you see something beautiful there?"

"Yes, sir."

"What are you called?"

"Bernadette."

"Bernadette what?"

"Soubirous."

"Your father?"

"François."

"Your mother?"

"Louise."

"Louise what?"

"Soubirous."

"No, her maiden name?"

"Castérot."

"Your age?"

"Thirteen or fourteen."

"Is it thirteen or is it fourteen?"

"I don't know."

"Do you know how to read or write?"

"No, sir."

"Don't you go to school?"

"Not often."

"What do you do?"

"I baby-sit my little brothers."

"Do you go to catechism classes?"

"Yes, sir."

"Have you made your first Communion?"

"No, sir."

"So, Bernadette, you see the Blessed Virgin?"

"I never said I saw the Blessed Virgin."

"Oh, so you saw nothing!"

"Oh, yes, I saw something."

"What did you see?"

"Something white."

"Some 'thing' or some 'one'?"

" 'Aquero' (That) has the form of a little girl."

"And 'Aquero' (That) did not say, 'I am the Blessed Virgin'?"

" 'Aquero' (That) did not tell me so."

"Well, that's what they say in town. It seems they even write it in the newspapers."

(Since what people or newspapers said was no business of hers, Bernadette said nothing.)

"When did you see her for the first time?"

"Market day at Tarbes."

"Good! February 11th, and what happened?" She told him while he wrote down all she said. The recital over, he pretended to read what he had written.

There were a number of things that had surprised him. One of them was that Bernadette spoke of her lady, not as a lady but as "Aquero" (That).

" 'Aquero' (That) has the form of a young lady— a beautiful young lady—like Mademoiselle Pailhaisson or Mademoiselle Dufo?" (two very pretty local belles).

"Oh! They'd never do!" Bernadette disgustedly answered.

The other piece of information that dilated his pupils and flared his investigative nostrils was the name of Madame Milhet—a very clever piece of baggage, that!

"Now, Madame Milhet took you to her house and told you what to say?"

"No. Yesterday I returned home."

"Why?"

"My aunt did not want me to go back there."

"Madame Milhet gave you a lot of money?"

"No, no money."

"Are you sure?"

"Very sure!"

"How many people have you told?"

"My sister Marie (Toinette) and Jeanne ('Baloum' Abadie)."

"What did they say?"

"They made fun of me."

"Who else?"

"My mother."

"What did she say?"

"She said I was dreaming and that I couldn't go back."

"Who else?"

"My Aunt Romaine Sajous."

"Who is she?"

"She lives upstairs over us."

"And what did she say?"

"It was an illusion."

"Who else?"

"Cyprine."

"Cyprine who?"

"Gesta."

Those Soubirous relatives weren't the greatest, thought Jacomet.

"Did you tell the nuns?"

"Yes, to the Superior and to the Sister who teaches us sewing."

"What did they say?"

" 'You were dreaming. Don't stop at such stuff.' "

"Yes," said Jacomet, "you were dreaming."

"No, I was wide awake."

"You thought you saw."

"No, I have seen 'Aquero' (That) a number of times. I can't always be mistaken."

"Yes, you're mistaken. Others are there, too; they have eyes and they see nothing."

"I can't explain that, but I'm sure I saw what I saw."

"Listen, Bernadette, everyone is laughing at you. They say that you are mistaken, that you are a fool. For your own good, you must not return to the grotto."

"But I promised to go for a fortnight."

"Since you were mistaken, you promised no one. Be reasonable, promise me you won't go back."

Bernadette was silent, but those limpid eyes of hers told Jacomet she was not about to break her promise. Not getting anywhere, Jacomet decided to try another track.

"I knew your story beforehand. Who fed this to you?"

"What do you mean?"

"Who told you of this beautiful lady at the grotto, and to repeat this story? Who promised you much if you kept repeating it?"

"No one."

"And who after that said it was the Blessed Virgin? You had better tell me, because I already know. I'm only doing this to see if you are going to be frank."

"Sir, I told you the truth."

"No, you are lying. I want to be quite clear. If you admit you're lying, we'll fix it up right here and nothing more will be said. If you don't, I'll take you to court."

Bernadette said nothing. Hoping to see tears, Jacomet was taken aback by the next words he heard:

"You can do what you want, sir."

"All the worse for you," he grumbled.

This cool little girl was irking him more than he cared to admit. Let's try something else.

"All right. I'm going to write down everything you said; then we'll see whether you are lying or not."

Flourishing a large sheet of paper, he began deliberately writing, and filled three sheets, hoping to wear down her stubbornness. She patiently watched him and waited. When he was finished, he read:

"Your name is Bernadette, aged thirteen or fourteen. On February 11th you went to the grotto...."

Bernadette listened intently. He read on:

"The Blessed Virgin appeared to me."

"I did not say it was the Blessed Virgin," she objected.

Jacomet lamely argued, "Why do people say it was the Blessed Virgin?" But continued, "A lady dressed in white, twenty years of age."

"No, I didn't say twenty years of age!"

"Beautiful, like Mademoiselle Pailhaisson...."

"Oh, no! I said prettier than all those ladies you named!"

"Her hair fell behind her like a veil...."

"No! Her hair could barely be seen."

Down the page he went, and at each misstatement Bernadette corrected him and finally protested, "You changed everything I told you!"

Here and there he insisted, "Yes, you said so."

"No, I did not," she countered.

"Yes, you did."

It was becoming a shouting match. Exasperated by her standing up to him, he veered his course:

"You make everyone chase after you."

"I told no one to go."

"Yes, you love to have everyone see you."

"No, I'm very tired of it all."

"If you are so tired of it all, say that you haven't seen a thing."

"But I did see!" Bernadette would not yield an inch.

The crowds outside, who had gathered when they heard that Bernadette had been taken to the house of the Police Superintendent, were getting restless and threatening. Thoroughly exhausted by his efforts, Jacomet would give it one last try:

"Are you going to admit you're lying?"

"I told you the truth, sir."

"I'll forget everything if you admit you saw nothing."

"Sir, I saw what I saw and cannot say otherwise."

"Well, at least you'll promise me that you won't go back to the grotto? Now, this is your last chance!"

"Sir, I promised to go back."

"All right, you asked for this. I'll send for the gendarmes. You're going to jail," and on saying this he marched out of the room.

Toward the end of the questioning, a local official and friend of Jacomet's, Jean Baptist

Estrade, quietly slipped into the room. When Jacomet had gone out, Estrade tried reasoning with Bernadette; but she, sensing he was interfering in matters not his business, remained silent.

Besides his frustration with Bernadette, Jacomet wanted to put a stop to the uproar outside his home. The crowd had increased, and when Bernadette's father joined them they pushed him to the forefront, egging him on to go in there to protect his daughter. In the midst of the hubbub, the door suddenly opened and there stood the Superintendent of Police, as big as life.

"I'm the girl's father," François meekly murmured.

"I'm glad to see you," said Jacomet, as he pulled François in and closed the door behind him. "I was about to send for you. This little game has gone on long enough. The girl is tired of all these people chasing after her. She's tired of being forced to go there...."

"Forced!" exclaimed François, "we're trying to stop her."

"Listen," said Jacomet, as he waved the last sheet he had scribbled on, "This is what she told me, crying as she said it: 'Papa and Mama are on the other side. It's up to you to forbid them from forcing me to go to the grotto. I'm tired and I don't want to go back.'"

The unlettered Francois stupidly looked at the sheet with all those mysterious hieroglyphics and could not believe what was just said to him. He would be perfectly happy to stop all this misery to him and to his family. With the upper hand now his, Jacomet pushed his advantage:

"You don't want to go back to prison, and I certainly wouldn't want to be the one to send you."

"Oh! We are sick of the whole thing. I am most happy to do as you ask. I'll close my door to people, and my daughter will not go back," Francois fervently promised.

Jacomet had succeeded with the father, where he had abysmally failed with the daughter; but even a poor victory would be some kind of salve to his wounded ego.

Father and daughter left by a side door, but the crowds were everywhere. "What did he say to you? What did he do?" they shouted. Bernadette, the calmest in the crowd, answered nothing. Seeing a smile on her face as they went homeward, someone asked her what amused her. Picturing to herself once more Jacomet in his rages, real or pretended, she answered, "He was trembling so much that the tassel on his calotte was dancing all over!"

The following day, Monday, February 22, was to be a sad one for Bernadette. Her parents, fearing Jacomet's reprisals, pounded into Bernadette's head that she was not to return to the grotto. She was an obedient child, and, cost what it would, she would obey. She went directly to school in the morning, but, returning to school in the afternoon, at the very gates of the Hospice something stronger than she pushed her to take the road to the grotto. The gendarmes were watching her, and took off after her. At the grotto she began the rosary and finished it, but the lady did not appear. The grapevine had spread the news that Bernadette was there, and one hundred people came to see. What had she done to displease her lady? Bernadette was crestfallen. The mockers were triumphant. Her godmother, Aunt Bernarde, dragged her away from her disgrace. So confused at her lady's nonappearance, she went back to see her confessor, the Abbé Pomian, who told her, "They have no right to stop you." Back home, her father, seeing her so downcast, and perhaps moved by what the Abbé Pomian had told her, lifted his prohibition.

The next day the lady reappeared, as she did again on the day after that. On these days Bernadette was beginning to do strange things: walking on her knees up to the grotto; kissing the ground; looking very sad and shedding tears. The vision over, she explained that the lady asked her to do the things she did as penances for the conversion of sinners. The mockers scoffed at all of this.

But Thursday, February 25, took the cake! During the vision Bernadette rose, went toward the Gave River, then, looking very puzzled, went back to a spot where she began scratching the earth. When muddy water appeared, she tried three times to put some in her mouth, but it was so repugnant to her, she threw it away. On her fourth try, she succeeded in swallowing some. She then daubed her face with some, and then chewed on some unsavory herbs growing there. The crowd thought she had gone mad.

The vision over, she explained that the lady had told her to go drink at the spring and to wash in it. Since there was no spring, she went to the Gave River; but the lady did not mean that. She pointed to a spot where Bernadette dug in the earth. When muddy water appeared Bernadette tried to drink some, but could not get herself to drink except on her fourth try. Since the lady wanted her to wash in it as well, she smeared her face with it. The lady also told her to eat the unsavory herbs. The mockers wouldn't believe a word of this. Even her staunchest believers had a hard time convincing themselves. It was only later that the people noticed that the water Bernadette had scratched into existence began as a trickle but soon became a clear streamlet, finding its way to the Gave River. People drank or washed in it and claimed it was miraculous; it cured them.

That evening it was the Imperial Prosecutor's turn to try to stop Bernadette. He called for her and, accompanied by her mother, she went to his office. There she underwent the same kind of interrogatory as the Superintendent of Police had conducted, but Vital Dutour, the Imperial Prosecutor, failed as miserably as the Superintendent had. She had promised the lady to go to the grotto for the fortnight, and she would keep her promise. Once again a menacing crowd had gathered to protest Bernadette's seizure. The Prosecutor thought it time to release her, but not before Bernadette gave him a lesson in manners. He had had Bernadette and her mother stand throughout his two hours of questioning, a very tiring experience for both. When he finally threatened to send them to jail, Bernadette's mother could literally stand no longer. Only then did the Prosecutor offer them chairs. Bernadette's mother could not refuse the offer, but Bernadette, who had felt the contempt the Prosecutor had for them, could not resist saying to him, "No, we'd dirty them!" and then sat, tailor-fashion, on the floor—as she reported years later.

In spite of the threats, Bernadette returned to the grotto on the next day, February 26, but that day was to be as sad as February 22nd; the lady did not appear. Once again Bernadette could not imagine what she had done to offend the lady.

The lady reappeared on each of the remaining days of the fortnight. During this time the lady told Bernadette to go to the priests and tell them she wanted a chapel built there at the grotto. The priests, to Bernadette, meant her pastor, Dean Dominique Peyramale.

The Dean was a blustery priest of forty-seven in 1858, who had won the hearts of his people during the cholera epidemic three years before. Like the Police Superintendent, Jacomet, he had devoted himself to the sick and dying and thereby earned himself a lasting place in their gratitude. He was not at all happy about all this traipsing back and forth to the grotto, and forbade the priests of his deanery to go there. He was a man to be obeyed; they did not go. Of all the people Bernadette had to deal with, he was the one who scared her most.

When she went to tell him of her lady's request for a chapel at the grotto, he went into a tirade. He called her a fake and a liar. He told her that she was a show-off, craving the attention of the crowds. When he had cooled down a bit, he asked her who this lady was; what was her name? The pastor of Lourdes would not deal with a nameless vision. Would the lady come up with the money to build this chapel? Bernadette could answer none of these questions. He then gave Bernadette a request of his own to bring back to the lady: have the lady make the rose bush bloom where the lady was standing.

At her next visit Bernadette told the lady of the pastor's demand, but all the Dean got for all his bluster was a smile from the lady. She ignored his demand but added another one of her own: she wanted processions at the grotto.

When Bernadette returned to tell the Dean of this, he had another temper-tantrum. He ranted about the fact that it was not up to him to build chapels or allow processions, but up to the bishop. He raved on that the pastor of Lourdes did not deal with a nameless vision, and went on and on. He finally shooed her out of his rectory with the order of not bothering him again.

Poor Bernadette! She had just left him when she remembered that the lady had repeated the request for a chapel, and this had completely slipped her mind. There was nothing else for her to do but go back. She dreaded going back alone, but neither her mother nor her Aunt Bernarde wanted to go with her. A neighbor, Dominiquette Cazenave, taking pity on her, said she would go along. She set up an appointment for seven that evening. The Dean, his two curates, Pène and Serres, and L'Abbé Pomian quizzed her closely. Once the interview was over, Bernadette felt the greatest relief. The one thing Bernadette gathered from all the Dean had said was that unless he knew the lady's name, there would be no chapel. She must get the lady to tell her who she was.

On the second to the last day of the fortnight there were about three thousand at the grotto when Bernadette arrived, but the lady did not appear. Only later in the day when Bernadette went back—there being only about one hundred then—did the lady appear. The last day of the fortnight, March 4, came and with it the largest of the crowds. There were about twenty thousand present, all with the greatest expectations: the lady would do something extraordinary, or at least would reveal who she was. They wanted to be in on the climax. They were doomed to disappointment; the lady did neither of the things they expected. But then, neither did she say good-bye to Bernadette, who, after this vision, resumed her usual routine and waited for the lady to call her again. The fortnight was over.

But not before a rekindling of the crowd's fervor for Bernadette. On her way to the grotto that morning a father had pleaded with her, "Pray for my child, who is blind!" His blind child, conspicuous in a red capulet, wore a band over her eyes. "Go, have her wash at the spring," Bernadette told him. After the vision, on her return home, Bernadette caught sight of the red capulet, and wanted to see the little girl again. When she was brought to her, Bernadette kissed her. The little girl was so happy that she held Bernadette's hand, and both girls expressed their happiness in peals of laughter. Bernadette gave her another big hug and left her. The little girl, Eugénie Troy, pulled off her bandage to see her new-found friend; and daylight, which had been intolerable up to now, gave her no trouble at all. "Miracle!" the crowd shouted; but it was only a remission of pain, happening at a moment of exuberance. A few weeks later her condition was as it had been. But this occurrence enthused the crowd almost to delirium. Bernadette was a "miracle-worker"; they must have her touch them or their beads and medals. Exhausted with the press of the crowd around her, Bernadette asked them, "And after I have touched them, what more will be added to them? Why touch me, I have no power?" It was all in vain; her modesty just fired them up all the more. Her touch was that of a saint.

Revelation

Ever since the fortnight of visions had begun, Bernadette was experiencing the start of the unhappiness her lady had warned her of in the third apparition. People would not let her alone. They wanted her to repeat, over and over again, what had happened during her visions; they called her a saint and wanted her to touch them or their medals and rosaries; they wanted snippets of her clothing or locks from her hair. Those who considered themselves close to her and the more brazen of the strangers wanted to hug and kiss her. There was no peace in the Rue des Petits Fossés; visitors tramped in and out of the *Cachot*, practically at will.

What was most surprising about all this is that none of it turned Bernadette's head. It irked her when people wanted her to bless their beads or medals. "I'm not a priest! I don't wear a stole!" was her reply to them. As for "souvenirs"—pieces of her clothing or locks from her hair—she thought the petitioners were crazy. Only the lady counted; she, herself, did not count at all. Why they could not see the lady as she did, nor hear the conversation they carried on between them in normal tones, she could not understand. When they tried to pry the three secrets and the prayer the lady had given her for herself alone, she was deft in evading their questions. One of her frequent answers was, "If I told you, they would not be secrets any more, would they?"

Bernadette quit going to the grotto after March 4, but people kept going in varying numbers. This was very disagreeable to the local officials. They called Bernadette in on March 18 for another question period. The panel was made up of the Imperial Prosecutor, Dutour; the Mayor, Lacadé; the Superintendent of Police, Jacomet; and the Mayor's secretary, Joanas. They repeated many of their previous questions, but were more interested in the cures Bernadette was supposed to have caused. She denied curing anyone, and, though she saw two sick or disabled people, they remained exactly as they were. At the end of the session she said, "I don't know whether I'll ever go back to the grotto." In his report Dutour interpreted this as: "She promised not to go back and not to lend herself to the abuses that gullibility and bad faith make of her actions and of her person." That was the official mind as of March 18.

A week later, on March 25, the feast of the Annunciation, Bernadette once again felt the urge to go to the grotto. She arrived before daybreak, yet there were about one hundred persons already there. When the lady appeared to her, she remembered the Dean's threat: "No name—no chapel!" She must get the lady to identify herself. Although she graciously asked the lady three times to tell her her name, all she got in reply was a smile. She just could not give up. She asked once more. This time the lady did not smile, but extended her arms down and outward, then joined her hands at her breast, raised her eyes to heaven, and said, "I am the Immaculate Conception."

The vision over, Bernadette was so happy that she wanted to leave something at the grotto, the candle she held, but it belonged to her Aunt Lucile. After getting her permission to leave it with the rest of the burning candles, she ran off to the rectory to tell the Dean what he had clamored for. Repeating the words over and over so that she would not forget them, she at last bounded into his room and said, "I am the Immaculate Conception." On hearing this, the Dean, raising himself to full height, was about to blast her for her colossal conceit, when she prevented him by saying, " 'Aquero' (That) said, 'I am the Immaculate Conception.' "

"A lady cannot bear that name!" exploded the Dean. He reasoned that the Virgin was conceived without sin. Her conception was Immaculate, but how could she say she was her own conception? "You are mistaken! Do you know what you are saying?" he asked. Bernadette shook her head. "Then how can you say this if you didn't understand?" he asked her. "I repeated it all along the way," said Bernadette. Bernadette had not forgotten his "No name—no chapel!" Now she reminded him, "She still wants the chapel." The Dean was flabbergasted; he needed time to think. "Go home," he told her. "I will see you another day."

Only in the afternoon did Bernadette learn what the words "Immaculate Conception" meant. She had always shown more common sense and more restraint than anyone else. She had never claimed that the apparition was the Blessed Virgin. She had not even called the vision a lady. She had called the vision "Aquero" (That). Now her common sense and self-restraint were rewarded: "Aquero" (That) was none other than the Blessed Virgin Mary.

After the 25th of March the believers could not contain their joy. They had known all along that it was the Virgin Mary who was hallowing their town by her visits to Bernadette. The state authorities were beside themselves with anger. Since the local officials had muffed their chances, Baron Massy, the Prefect of the Hautes Pyrenées, decided to have Bernadette examined by competent doctors, in view of having her committed. Doctors Balencie, Lacrampe, and Peyrus examined her but could find nothing radically wrong with her. In spite of their findings, they would find the means to accomplish what the Prefect wànted.

People, both of low and high degree, continued to bombard her with questions. One of the latter, Albert de Rességuier, a former Member of the Assembly, put her through a minute examination in the presence of Dean Peyramale, who wrote to the bishop of Tarbes concerning it: "Everything about the girl deeply impressed him. He subjected her to a most detailed line of questioning, but the child answered all his questions with ability far above her age level, and, what seemed to me, far above her intelligence."

The only specific item of the questionnaire that has come down to us is about the language the Blessed Virgin spoke with Bernadette. "It was patois" (the dialect of the region), Bernadette told him. He objected to that: "The Blessed Virgin could not have spoken patois. God and the Blessed Virgin don't speak that language," he categorically told her. As learned as he was, Bernadette's reply left him mute. "How come we know it, if they don't?"

In the same letter the Dean gave the bishop another of Bernadette's outspoken answers. Before a group of brilliantly attired young ladies, Bernadette was asked if the lady was beautiful. "Oh, yes!" she answered, and turning toward the young ladies added, "Much prettier than all of these!"

On the 28th of March the three Tardhivail sisters questioned Bernadette on the doctors' examination, only to learn that she feared none of these gentlemen, nor the prosecutor, nor the superintendent of police. "Suppose they put you in jail?" they asked. "It's all the same to me!" was her answer.

Candle Miracle

On April 7 Bernadette felt drawn to the grotto once more. Arriving there at 5:30 in the morning, she knelt and began to say her beads. A crowd was already there. Blazy, a wine merchant, had furnished her with a long, heavy candle, so heavy she rested it on the ground. When the Virgin appeared Bernadette went into ecstasy. Unaware of what was going on about her, she was oblivious of the candle flame playing on her hands, which she had cupped at the top of the candle to prevent the wind from blowing it out. People cried, "She's burning herself!" but Doctor Dozous, a local doctor, would allow no one to correct the situation. Although the flame had been in contact with her hands for about fifteen minutes, when Doctor Dozous examined her hands after the vision, he found them perfectly sound. He then and there joined the ranks of the believers. Everyone who saw what had happened called this "The Miracle of the Candle."

To protect her from the curious crowd, two of the Tardhivail sisters took Bernadette to their home, but they proved more curious still, because they tried putting a lighted candle to her hands. She quickly pulled hands away, crying, "You're burning me!" On leaving them she ran into Madame Garoby, who tried the same experiment. All Bernadette could think was that everyone was going crazy!

On May 29, a priest, the Abbé Vincent Péré, gave her a rough quiz. Because he was not of the region he did not consider himself bound by the Dean's order for priests to stay away from the grotto. After going to the grotto he visited Bernadette and questioned her harshly, calling her a liar and a little hussy. He tried to convince her that she was mistaken, that he, himself, had thought he heard rustling sounds at the grotto. What she heard was some bird nesting there. "If it was a bird, he wouldn't have spoken," replied Bernadette. As always, a group of people gathered to listen to what was going on, workmen among them, who became very angry at his torturing Bernadette. Before things got nasty he thought it wise to leave.

On June 3, Bernadette made her First Communion with her class at the Hospice of Lourdes. Emmanuélite Estrade asked her the next day which had given her more pleasure, receiving Holy Communion or her visions of the Blessed Virgin. Bernadette answered, "These two things go together, and they cannot be compared. I was very happy in both."

Two days after making her First Communion, Bernadette received help from an altogether surprising and unexpected source, from none other than Dean Peyramale himself. The Mayor of Lourdes, Lacadé, and the Public Prosecutor, Dutour, came to him for support regarding the new trespass laws at the grotto. He went along with that; but when the Mayor advised him of what the Prefect had in mind for Bernadette, he strenuously objected. There was nothing mentally wrong with Bernadette, he told them; and, furthermore, if they tried to carry out their ill-conceived plan, it would be over his dead body. Taking care of Bernadette was easy enough, but tangling with the redoubtable Dean was not a thing to look forward to; they did not want a revolt on their hands. When the Prefect received the report of the interview from the Mayor, he wisely scuttled the plan.

Since the Lady had given her name to Bernadette on March 25, the Dean had second thoughts about this child's persistence in her claims and about her natural modesty. He had called her a liar, a fake, and a show-off, but he was beginning to reverse his judgment. The greatest liar in the world could never be so consistent in telling what she had to tell and with no variations in the repeated tellings. Besides, her unassuming ways went directly to his pastoral heart. Henceforth he would be her champion.

He continued to object to the attention people lavished on her, but there was not too much he could do about it. He wondered how long she could stay as innocent and modest as she was, for, in his experience, no one could remain immune to all the blandishments of so many, so often poured out. There might be a way of safeguarding her humility, but he would have to delay putting it into execution.

Troubles

To understand the reaction of the unbelievers and the skeptics to Bernadette and Lourdes, the events of the last sixty years in France have to be taken into consideration. The French Church in 1858 was not the church it had been. Once called "The Eldest Daughter of the Church," France was now in a pretty bedragled state. In 1858 it was only about sixty years since the Revolution in 1789, followed by The Terror and The Directory. It was only forty years since Napoleon, with his wars, his exile, and his return. The Bourbons returned to power with Louis XVIII, followed by Louis Philippe and his deposition. The Second Republic was proclaimed only to be quickly followed by the Second Empire under Napoleon III in 1852. During those years the leaders of the people had persecuted the Church by taking the Pope into captivity, destroying the power of the Bishops, closing churches and schools by doing away with most religious orders, and banishing all priests who did not take the oath to sustain the government. In a word, the give-and-take between the Church and the government had given way to the government wanting full power over the Church. In 1858, when Bernadette had her visions, the last thing the government wanted was an apparition from another world.

To the government, all the gatherings at the grotto were against the law; the people were starting a cult without the state's sanction. On May 4 the Prefect had all candles and other religious articles removed. On June 7 he had the Mayor of Lourdes close the grotto. Barricades were put up on the 15th of June, only to be torn down on July 4. They were rebuilt on July 10. Trespassers were arrested. The people gave the officials a very difficult time, until Dean Peyramale advised his parishioners to obey the new laws. This did not entirely do away with the problem; some people continued regularly to gather outside the barricades to pray, and continued to steal the water from the spring Bernadette had scratched into existence. This hassle was to go on until October 2, when a memorandum from the Emperor Napoleon III, himself, allowed everyone access to the grotto.

The Lady's Good-Bye

As the weeks went by and Bernadette quit going to the grotto, the officials relaxed their watch over her activities. Three months had passed since her last vision, when the irresistible urge to go to the grotto gripped her once more. The Virgin chose her Feast of Mount Carmel, July 16, to say good-bye to Bernadette. Since the barricades had been rebuilt for the third time July 10, and since the new laws were in full force, what was Bernadette to do? She waited until sunset, and went disguised in a large cape that hid three quarters of her diminutive figure. With her Aunt Lucile, she took the road to the Ribère field across the Gave River. A few small groups were there when she arrived. She knelt and almost immediately went into ecstasy, her face radiating the happiness she was experiencing.

After the vision she said that the Virgin was more beautiful than she had ever seen her. Asked what the Blessed Virgin said, she answered, "Nothing." Just seeing her was contentment enough for Bernadette. One of the

Tardhivail sisters, who was there, asked her how she could see, what with the distance and the barricades. "I saw neither the planks nor the Gave," she answered, "it seems to me that I was at the grotto, with no more distance than at other times. I saw nothing but the Virgin." How Bernadette knew this was to be the last time she was to see the Virgin, she never explained.

This last visit to the grotto was kept very quiet, so quiet that Jacomet and his gendarmes never got wind of it. No little girl could attract so much attention without others trying to share the limelight. A rash of fake visionaries cropped up, all claiming they had seen the Blessed Virgin. Bernadette had been more than the public officials could stand; they were not going to suffer any more visionaries. On a visit to Lourdes, Baron Massy, on May 4, issued an edict, stating that whoever proclaimed himself or herself a visionary would immediately be arrested and detained in the Hospice of Lourdes (in the mental patients' ward, presumably!). Strictly speaking, they could have picked up Bernadette at any time, because she made no excuses for her visions. Those in charge of her sent her off to Cauterets for health reasons, it seems, but more plausibly to get her away from the jaundiced eyes of the public officials.

The Messenger

Bernadette had accomplished what the Blessed Virgin had asked: she had discovered the miraculous spring and had delivered to the priests the orders to have a chapel built at the grotto and to have processions there. The spring was merrily gurgling, but the chapel and the processions were still floating ideas. The only one who could make these become a reality was the bishop of Tarbes, Bishop Bertrand Laurence, a dour man who used his words sparingly. He had been kept posted on all that was going on in Lourdes. Twelve days after the last apparition, he set up a commission to test the validity of all claims. Included in his commission were a number of clergymen and a group of expert laymen, hydrologist, chemists, geologists, and so on. They were to sit in judgment for the next three years.

One of the first witnesses the commission had to call had to be the star witness, Bernadette. In spite of the formality of the investigation, the minuteness of the questionings and the awesomeness of the investigators, Bernadette never deviated from what she had always told of her visions. These examiners tried to the best of their canonical and legal minds to catch her in a lie, but after exhaustive grillings they had to admit defeat; Bernadette was no liar. Despite laws and barricades, they visited the grotto and conducted a thorough investigation of the scene of the apparitions.

The spring had caused all kinds of problems to the local officials. Some people using the water claimed it cured them, and, since there were a number of cures that the doctors could not explain, the officials had to find reasons for these cures. The Mayor of Lourdes had a chemist friend of his from Tarbes analyze the water. He gave it a very high rating, raising the Mayor's hopes of making Massabielle a rival to Cauterets, Luz, and Barèges, spas in the region. Pailhaisson, a local pharmacist, possibly seeing his business dwindling, attacked everything the Mayor's friend had said. The water was finally analyzed by Professor Filhol of the Faculty of Science in Toulouse, who said the water was plain, ordinary, spring water. It was not a mineral spring at all—thus dashing all of the Mayor's hopes—and his report went on to say that the water could be drunk without harmful effects.

Bernadette had become an instant celebrity, at the beck and call of any and everyone who wanted to interview her; and the interviews multiplied. From the start of her visions, she would never again be able to call her life her own. How many times Bernadette had to tell her visions, no one knows; but someone has estimated that, whether to individuals or to groups, large and small, she told her experiences to some 30,000 people. No matter the count, she did have to tell her story to many, many people, many, many times. Keeping in mind that she was an asthmatic, not physically strong, it is amazing to see how she stood up to this barrage of questions day after day. What gave her the strength to carry on was her belief that she was the Blessed Virgin's messenger, and, cost what it might, she had to keep repeating the message.

Visitors to see Bernadette came and went; some enthralled with her recital, others trying to prove her a fake. Whoever they were, Bernadette acted courteously toward all except when they tried to force gifts upon her or when they showed utter disbelief. She accepted no gifts from anyone, and as for the unbelievers, she did not think it her duty to make believers of them.

A wealthy woman visited her and fell under her charm, but when she tried to slip a roll of gold coins in her hand it was as though she had put a red hot poker there instead. Bernadette jumped up and the roll of gold coins fell to the floor; then, noticing the distress this caused the surprised woman, she gently returned it to her. Nothing could get her to accept gifts.

The Bishop of Montpelier, Bishop Thibault, came to see her and wanted to do something for her. He tried to give her his golden chain rosary, but she said, "I already have a rosary." "How about swapping rosaries, then?" the bishop said. "No, thank you, I prefer my own." Then, seeing him embarrassed, she added, "Yours is good for you, but thank you very much."

Father Nègre, a Jesuit priest, tried to convince her that it was the devil in disguise who had appeared to her, but her answers were much more convincing than his arguments.

Many others like Father Nègre tried to dissuade her in her claims, but she would smile pleasantly at them, say nothing if she thought that was the best way to treat these people, and let her limpid eyes do her talking. Her silences were as loud as her talk.

Many of the interviewers were intrigued with the three secrets the Blessed Virgin had given her, for her alone, and tried directly or by ruse to extract them from her—always unsuccessfully. Her answers would vary.

"Would you tell them to the Pope?"

"He does not need to know them." (Or, "The Lady told me to tell no one; the Pope is a person, isn't he?" Or, "If the Blessed Mother tells me to, I'll tell him.")

"Are they about your vocation to the sisterhood?"

"Oh! More serious than that!"

"Do they pertain to the Church?"

"No! They pertain to me alone."

One rash priest demanded to know them, telling her as a priest he had the right to know them. All he got for his bluster was a pathetic smile. And Bernadette went to the grave without revealing those secrets to anyone.

One of the things that puzzled many was her rejection of all gifts, in spite of the fact that she and her family lived below the poverty level. The knowledge of this was so widespread that when the officials tried blackening her name with the accusation that she was making money from her "shenanigans" at the grotto, the people treated the accusation with the contempt it deserved. Neither would she allow her family to batten on her grotto fame. She boxed her little brother's ears for accepting coins from some well-wisher. She made him return the money; the ear-boxing was to remind him not to do it again.

A journalist, Balech de Lagarde, from the *Courier Francais* tried to tempt her.

"Listen, Bernadette, you have to come to Paris with me, and in three weeks you'll be rich. I will take care of your fortune."

"Oh, no! I want to stay poor."

"That makes no sense. I don't mean you'll come along with me alone; your parents will come along, too. You won't have to leave them...."

"You're talking for nothing. I don't want to."

"60,000 francs or 100,000 francs. That's a fortune!"

"Don't talk like that, or I'm going home."

And Bernadette meant exactly what she said.

The Hospice

The doctors who had gone to the *Cachot* to examine Bernadette had warned François and Louise that they would have to move out of that pest hole if they wanted to save the children they had. About the middle of September, 1858, François was able to move his family out. They had lived there for almost two years. Bernadette's little brother, Justin, was to live seven more years, but that kind of existence caught up with the little boy, for he died at ten.

The public officials were not the only ones keeping an eye on Bernadette; so, too, was Dean Peyramale. The kind of life Bernadette was leading was not at all to his liking. All the attention that was being forced on her would spoil her. Something would have to be done. He had tried to separate her from her family shortly after the visions were over, but both she and her parents demurred and nothing was done about it. Now, two years later, this could not go on.

On the 5th of February, 1860, Bernadette was confirmed by Bishop Laurence of Tarbes. It was the first time the Bishop met her.

Bernadette was now sixteen and could not spend the rest of her life baby-sitting children. On a visit from Dominiquette Cazenave, the woman who had accompanied her on one of her formidable visits to the Dean, Bernadette's mother asked her if she would give Bernadette sewing lessons. "Not here!" said Dominiquette, knowing all too well of the constant interruptions in the Soubirous household. "Let her come to my house, where there's quiet." For such a change it was necessary to get the Dean's permission, since he regulated all major changes in Bernadette's way of life. Dominiquette went to see him and ended by saying to him, "You can't leave her in the world!" The Dean was in perfect accord and decided to try his plan once more: to place her in the Hospice of Lourdes, where the Sisters of Nevers would supervise her. These Sisters did not only operate a hospital at the hospice, but a day and boarding school as well. Mayor Lacadé agreed with the Dean. She would be entered free, as a sick person unable to pay, but not sick enough not to be able to pursue her education. The superior consented to the arrangement.

Bernadette moved into the Hospice July 15, 1860, and was to live there for the next six years. She was to be allowed to visit her parents freely, but with a nun accompanying her. She was not allowed to visit anywhere else, except with the express permission of the Dean; and, at the Hospice, visitors were not allowed to see her, unless the Dean or the sisters granted them permission.

This was the first time in her life that Bernadette would attend classes regularly. Her size played in her favor; she was sixteen but looked eleven, and in a class of youngsters of eleven or twelve she fitted in admirably. Learning to read, write, and do sums did not come easily to her, but though her classmates suggested they do her work for her, she was quick enough to see that sister would recognize the switch and would scold her. She took to sewing with nimble fingers, and had a natural flair for embroidery.

What surprised the sisters and her classmates alike was her liveliness. They expected her to be a sort of plaster-saint, which she definitely was not. Doctor Balencie had prescribed snuff for her asthma. When a section of the class took a sneezing fit one day, the sister in charge was aghast to learn that the culprit behind this was Bernadette, who had passed her snuff box around. She was as spirited in recreations as all the rest, only she got winded more easily. Because of this she could not jump rope, but liked to turn the rope for others to jump. She once threw one of her sabots out the window so that ten-year-old Julie Garros could go out to fetch it, bringing back some of the ripe strawberries that caused her to throw her sabot out in the first place. She shocked Sister Victorine Poux, who had her in special charge, when she found Bernadette trying to flounce her dress to give it a stylish look. And, worse still, putting an enlarger (a block of wood!) inside her corset as a filler. The sisters and her classmates watched her like hawks, and any deviation from what they thought should be her conduct was never let to pass.

When it came to her prayer life, all impishness ceased. She was very recollected at

Mass and could not understand how some girls could read the romances of the day, hidden behind their missals. Her signs of the cross continued as beautiful as the Virgin had taught her to make them. She said her rosary often during the day, and fell asleep nightly saying it. Her confessor, the Abbé Pomian, allowed her to receive Communion every Sunday and sometimes during the week, an exceptional privilege at the time.

Though the Dean's plan to sequester her was a good one, it did not work out too well. Too many people were allowed to see her, and that almost daily. They came from all over, and easily got permission from the Dean or from the sisters. In the classroom her desk was near the door so that her frequent calls to the parlor would not disturb the other students. Calls came during class or during recreation, and she hated them all. She admitted one day that she preferred her asthma crises to receiving visits, but went to the parlor because of obedience to her superiors. Sister Victorine tells of seeing her shed big tears at the door before entering the parlor where twenty, thirty, or forty people awaited her. "Courage!" Sister told her, reminding her that the apparitions had not been for her sole pleasure, but for others. "The poor girl would wipe her eyes, and went in, giving all a gracious bow, and answered all their questions. After these ordeals she would return to the classroom or recreation as though nothing had happened," concluded sister.

Had it only been the questionings it would have been bad enough, but people wanted her to bless religious articles, or at least to touch them, or they wanted souvenirs from her, or they wanted her to autograph holy pictures. They treated her as a miracle worker, a most repugnant thing to her. When her confessor forbade her to touch articles, it was a pleasure for her to answer the blessing-seekers by saying, "I'm forbidden to do that."

Even her contempt for money took a new turn. At home she had refused all gifts, but now the gifts were for the Hospice. She still did all she could not to come in contact with them. She would tell people to put their money in the chapel poor-box, or if she had to take it she quickly gave it to the sister who was present at these visits.

It is a wonder that all the praise, flattery and adulation people gave her did not turn her head, but she took no pride or self-satisfaction in any of this. At the same time Dean Peyramale was the first of many of her superiors who often humiliated her publicly so that she would not become conceited. She felt these humiliations keenly but always thought them necessary. She admitted the favors she received were not merited; and toward the end of her life feared she had never appreciated them enough and would be judged for her failure.

To add to her popularity, after more than three years of investigating, the Bishop's Commission, set up to examine all claims pertaining to the Lourdes Question, delivered their verdict on January 18, 1862:

"We hold that the Immaculate Mary, Mother of God, actually appeared to Bernadette Soubirous on the eleventh of February, 1858, and on subsequent days, to the numer of eighteen, in the grotto of Massabielle, near the town of Lourdes; that the apparitions bear all the signs of authenticity and that the faithful are free to consider it true."

The Bishop of Tarbes then issued the following:

"In order to conform to the wish of the Blessed Virgin, several times expressed at the time of the apparitions, we propose to build a sanctuary on the ground adjoining the grotto, which has now become the property of the Diocese of Tarbes."

The Lady's request to have a chapel built at the grotto was about to be fulfilled, making Bernadette very happy. The other request, for processions, would follow in due course.

Bernadette's health continued frail. Sister Victorine Poux lists her ailments: toothaches, rheumatism in one leg, a painful shoulder that caused her to faint one Good Friday, an habitual cough, frequent spitting up of blood, occasional palpitations, and frequent asthma crises when they would bring her to the window to allow her to breathe. At these crises she would plead, "Open my chest!" Sister Victorine concludes her list by saying, "Though an habitual sufferer, she remained patient in all her sufferings, so much so that no one would have suspected her pains unless they knew her very well."

Her poor health never extracted pity from those who insisted they see her. During the summer vacations the visitors increased by the hundreds. Eight priests came to the Hospice to see her. The superior tried easing Bernadette's burden by saying, "There were already many visitors today, and more yesterday—more than nine hundred people!"—but they refused to take the hint. The superior allowed them to question Bernadette. After a theological argument among themselves on the way a glorified body speaks, they appealed to Bernadette. "I heard her very well," she answered. "Was it interior or sensible?" one asked. "Sensible," she answered. Then more and more questions that must have seemed silly to Bernadette. "Did her feet touch the ledge?" "There was moss where she stood that prevented me from seeing." After a coughing spell of hers, Bernadette was asked, "Do you sleep well?" "Yes," she answered, then smilingly added, "except when I cough." "Didn't you think you ought to tell your confessor the secret the Virgin gave you?" With a smile to remind the priest that one is obliged to tell sins alone to one's confessor, "It wasn't a sin!" she answered.

According to her brother, Jean-Marie, the family was often called to the Hospice when she had violent asthma attacks. One of these, worse than the others, happened on April 28, 1862. Doctor Balencie and a consultant arrived to examine her. Her confessor anointed her and gave her viaticum—a small particle of the host in Lourdes water; they were all sure she was dying. After the reception of Holy Communion, she began to breathe freely, as though a mountain had been removed from her chest, she explained. The following day Doctor Balencie paid her a visit and congratulated himself on the proper medicine he had prescribed. Bernadette told him she hadn't taken any medicine. "Well, well, you weren't as sick as we thought you were," he lamely replied. During her short lifetime Bernadette was to see doctors many times; her confidence in them was not great. After this particular instance, she said, "If I am sick again, I'll ask the doctor to be very careful—he mistook my sickness—I could have 'caved in.' "

It was also during her Hospice stay that Bernadette became acquainted with photographers. It certainly was none of her doing. Photography was only in its infancy; Daguerre had just discovered it five years before she was born. Though an amateur photographer, L'Abbé Bernadou took surprisingly good pictures of Bernadette, after getting the Dean's permission to pose her. He wanted her "in ecstasy," and fretted and fumed for the desired pose. She gave him a perfect squelch, "It's because She isn't here!" Three other photographers at that time were to seek and get the bishop's consent to take pictures of her, not at all out of altruistic motives. They were selling her pictures, which were a hot article. Told that her picture was being sold for ten centimes, her reaction was, "That's more than I'm worth!"

In the middle of 1863, some wealthy sisters from Lyons wanted a more dignified statue at the grotto of Lourdes to replace the plaster statuette people had placed there. They were ready to spend 7000 francs, plus the sculptor's expenses, for a new statue. They even suggested the sculptor, Joseph Fabisch, who had done the statues of Our Lady of La Salette and the Virgin of Fouvière. If he thought he had troubles executing these statues, he was in for a lot more. This statue was to be sculptured according to the details Bernadette would furnish. She was impossible to please when it came to her Lady; nothing on earth could adequately represent what she had seen. She did not want to hurt the artist's sensibilities, but what else could she do when he was so far from the reality? When the statue was completed and Bernadette saw it for the first time, her deep disappointment could only be expressed in what she said: "That isn't it, at all."

Time was slipping by and though Bernadette, when she was well, was busy with the constant stream of visitors; with her own much interrupted studies; with helping sick people in the Hospice; and occasionally taking care of the smallest pupils at the school, her life was taking no particular direction. She, herself, would have been perfectly happy to stay indefinitely at the Hospice, if only the rash of visitors could be stemmed.

Her Lady had not told her what to do once the visions were over; she could only wait and pray. She had been taken to the Carmel in Bagnères and had been deeply impressed with the hiddenness of their way of life, but at the same time she knew her health could never take the rigors of the cloister. Though she was told that exceptions could be made in certain cases, that did not suit her; if she could not follow the rule as the rest, she would have nothing to do with it. Dean Peyramale had once suggested the Sisters of Nevers, who were taking care of her at the Hospice, but, at the time, she knew her illiteracy and her health would deny her admission to any congregation. Among her visitors were many nuns from different congregations who tried to entice her to their congregations, but uselessly. Two reasons drew her to the Sisters of Nevers: the care of a few old patients at the Hospice the sisters let her tend, which awakened in her pity to tend the sick, and the fact that the Sisters of Nevers tried in no way to influence her choice.

Her plans for the future advanced a big step the day Bishop Forcade of Nevers came to the Hospice to see her. He unwittingly won her affection when he used her dialect to quell her excessive bell-ringing to announce his presence. "Prou! Prou!" ("Enough! Enough!") he told the bellringer, not knowing it was Bernadette. She returned to the kitchen, laughing merrily at the thought that he had used the dialect of her region. Later, when he interviewed her privately, he was very impressed by her answers concerning her visions. At the end of their conversation, he queried her about her future. As far as she was concerned her future was right here at the Hospice. He informed her that that could not last, unless she joined the sisters, since she was a charity case and, as a young lady, could not be supported forever. She objected that she did not have the postulant's dowry, to which he answered that any poor girl with a vocation needn't produce the dowry. She countered with the fact that she was good for nothing, to which he said that they would find something for her to do. To all this she said that she would have to think it over.

On April 4, 1864, Bernadette came to her final decision to join the Sisters of Nevers, when she told Mother Alexandrine Roques, then superior of the Hospice, that she wanted to be one of them. A number of delays were to postpone her entrance, sickness being the most important.

Her cousin, Jeanne Védère, to whom she had always been close, got permission from the Dean to take her to Momères, where Jeanne taught school. The Dean was very glad to accommodate her, as his brother was a doctor there and could take care of her if she should get sick. That visit stretched out to seven weeks.

Dufour, the photographer, learning of her stay in Momères, could not let such a golden opportunity pass. He got the bishop's permission to take new poses of her. He wanted to do this ultra-professionally, using scenic backdrops and other photographic techniques. He also wanted Bernadette to have changes of dress. This, her cousin told him, would not be Bernadette. He agreed. But, to see what Bernadette thought of this, Jeanne told her that Dufour wanted her to change her costume. Her quick retort was, "If Mr. Dufour does not find me pretty enough, tell him to leave me alone. I shall be all the happier that way. Let him be satisfied with my dress; I won't add a single pin to it."

Bernadette was happy to hear that she had been accepted as a postulant with the Sisters of Nevers, but her health gave her more problems. Visitors kept bothering her, and the crush of the crowds was the reason she was rarely allowed to go to the grotto. With the favorable answer from the superiors at Nevers, she began her postulancy, following the regimen of the sisters at the Hospice, insofar as her health would allow her.

When the Bishop of Tarbes, Bishop Laurence, wanted her to be present at the inauguration of the crypt, the substructure of what would one day be the chapel the Lady had requested, this caused another delay. At this celebration the sisters tried to hide Bernadette in the midst of the Children of Mary, all dressed alike, but the crowds were so avid to see and touch her that on their discovery of who she was, the sisters had great difficulty in trying to protect her. A group of soldiers present were called upon for help, and only with the greatest maneuvering were they able to fend off the crowd. Back at the Hospice, to quiet the people who had followed, Bernadette had to be marched up and down the garden so that they could see her. She considered this being shown off like a prize bull, a very disgusting experience. This celebration fired the minds of brand new crowds, who had never been to

Lourdes before; and this renewed interest in Bernadette determined those in charge to remove her from Lourdes as soon as possible. Whether or not a proposal of marriage added to their determination is not known, but there was such a proposal. The pining suitor was an intern from Nantes, who wished to bestow on Bernadette the high-sounding name of Raoul de Choisne de Tricqueville. He carried on a correspondence with the bishop of Tarbes, whom he reasoned was the proper authority to address in such a delicate matter. His last letter finds him languishing with pangs of unrequited love:

"It seems to me that I have nothing better to do than to get married, and I would hope to marry Bernadette. If I don't marry her I think I'll leave the world and ask God for the favor to die in solitude.... I am grateful for the way in which you told me the truth without sparing my feelings. I submit my judgment to yours. I did not think my desires could be harmful to a work wanted by the Blessed Virgin...."

Raoul de Choisne de Tricqueville may have come back to the charge when Bernadette was in Nevers, or it may have been another suitor. Whoever it was contacted the bishop of Nevers, Bishop Forcade, on the same useless errand. Bernadette may have been oblivious of her ardent admirer(s), but if she learned of the matter her reaction would have been the same as it was when the bishop of Nevers had suggested such a possibility to her when she was still at the Hospice of Lourdes. Her answer then was a vehement "Ah! As for that, never!"

On July 2, she had to submit to another picture-taking session, this time by Philippe Viron, who had obtained all the necessary permissions. He had her pose with the Sisters of the Hospice, first in her own costume, then in the habit of the congregation; then in a "friendship chain" with the Children of Mary; then with all of her maternal relatives; then with her paternal relatives; and three of herself, alone. That evening he wanted to present her with twelve pictures as a gift, but she wanted to pay for them; otherwise she felt they really would not belong to her. All she wanted them for was to give them away to relatives and friends before she left. Never one to accumulate possessions, she gave away the few she had: two books to two of the Hospice sisters, and a few rosary beads and medals to relatives and friends.

She visited the grotto for the last time, and, though it was a wrenching experience for her, her Aunt Basile reports that she suffered it bravely.

The night before she left, she stayed late at her family's home, and on leaving had to undergo another round of goodbyes from a crowd awaiting her outside. The next morning she bade her family a very tearful farewell at the Hospice, she being the only dry-eyed one there, according to her Aunt Basile. There must have been a strong tug at her heart strings on July 4, 1866, when the coach galloped away from all that she held dear: her family, her friends, and her beloved grotto. On the coach with her to

Tarbes were her godmother, Aunt Bernarde, her sister Toinette, and Sister Victorine Poux (who were to take the return coach to Lourdes), and. Mother Alexandrine Roques, the superior of the Hospice (who was to go the whole journey to Nevers). Bernadette left Lourdes in a blue dress someone had given her. Once she would have refused such a gift, but now she was a postulant and had to bow to the wishes of her superiors. At Tarbes they met the superior of the Hospice of Bagnères, Mother Ursula Court, with her postulant, Marie Larotis; and they all boarded the train together. They stopped once more to pick up the other Lourdes postulant, Léontine Mouret, and they were on their way again.

They stayed over at Bordeaux from Wednesday night to Friday noon. Their time was spent in visiting convents, one of which impressed Bernadette by its grandeur ("one would say a palace rather than a religious house," she later wrote), and the Carmelites' Church. They also gawked at the ships in the harbor and visited the Botanical Gardens, where the goldfish caught her eye. The way these little multicolored fish swam around, undisturbed by the little boys intently watching them, struck her as a real novelty, about which she later wrote to the sisters of the Hospice of Lourdes.

One last stopover at Périgueux. There she was shown off at St. Ursula's, where the teachers and students gathered in the parlor to see her; then at the "Misericorde," an orphanage for little girls. Always interested in tiny creatures, Bernadette caressed the tiniest of them. They slept in the hospital that night, but not before the vicar of the cathedral, L'Abbé Plantier, came to question her on the beauty of the Blessed Virgin.

At ten o'clock in the morning they took the train for the last lap of their journey, arriving at Nevers at 10:30 in the evening of the same day, July 7, 1866.

One stage of her life was over; a new one was about to begin.

New Arrival

Bernadette was finally at the motherhouse of the Sisters of Nevers. She had had her problems in making up her mind to join the sisters; the sisters had had their difficulties accepting her. Had their congregation not been a diocesan congregation, where the bishop of the diocese had the last word, it is doubtful that Bernadette would have been accepted. The bishop did not have an easy time persuading the superiors that Bernadette ought to be one of them. Bernadette was not one of your run-of-the-mill aspirants to the sisterhood; she had quite a past history. It was this that worried the superiors. They did not consider Bernadette a prize catch.

The works of their congregation included nursing the sick in hospitals and teaching in schools. Bernadette was a sickly girl, suffering from bouts of asthma, whose education was minimal. Where would she fit into the congregation? A sickly, semi-illiterate girl would be of no practical use.

To compound the superior's problem, Bernadette was a visionary of world fame. Who isn't a bit leery of visionaries? In Bernadette's case, she claimed to have seen the Blessed Virgin eighteen times and to have spoken to her during many of these visions. In a way they were private visions—Bernadette was the only one to see and hear the Virgin; but they were most public in another way—thousands of people had seen Bernadette during these visions. Not only that, but everything Bernadette had reported had come to pass. The Virgin wanted a chapel; she had it. The Virgin wanted processions at the grotto; she had them. The Virgin wanted Bernadette to drink at a seemingly nonexistent spring and to wash in it; Bernadette had done what she was told to do, and, now, the spring was merrily flowing, and the people were imitating Bernadette and calling the spring miraculous; it cured them. Four years after the visions, a bishop's commission had declared the visions true and worthy of belief by the faithful. Bernadette was the darling of thousands (and a fraud to other thousands). Hadn't all this attention affected her? If it had, how long would she last in a convent?

And wasn't it true that just when Bernadette made up her mind to join them that an asthma attack struck her so violently, she had to be anointed? Happening when it did, this convinced the superiors all the more that she would be a useless member of their congregation. But she recovered, and the bishop put a little more pressure on the superiors, and, willy-nilly, they gave in, more because the bishop was forcing their hand than because they thought Bernadette would be an acquisition to their congregation. Might not the bishop be forcing the hand of Providence as well?

When word spread in the motherhouse at Nevers that Bernadette had been accepted, can you imagine the commotion? Everyone knew of Bernadette, now they were going to meet her; they were consumed with curiosity. The nearer the day of her arrival approached, the more excited the sisters became. The superiors thought Bernadette had received enough attention already; they would have to nip this in the bud. They decided that on July 8th, the day after her arrival, they would have her publicly give an account of her visions; then they would forbid her to mention the grotto again. They would make the subject taboo to all the members of the community. They alone would judge when and to whom she could speak of the grotto.

As they decided, so it happened. The whole community, plus some visiting sisters—about 300 in all—assembled in the novices' conference room, and, in their midst, Bernadette, tired from her recent journey, told her story. When she got to the part where the Lady told her to drink of the spring water, she related how she threw it away three times before she could get herself to swallow some. The superior of the Hospice of Lourdes, who had been one of her traveling companions, Mother Alexandrine Roques, leaned over to another sister and said, "From that you can judge how little her spirit of mortification was!" Bernadette's keen ear caught the remark, and she protested, "But the water was so dirty!" When it came to the day the Lady revealed herself and Bernadette's imitation of her saying, "I am the Immaculate Conception," there was not a sister in the room who was not carried away. The superiors could have their own opinions, the rest of the sisters thought Bernadette wonderful.

She then had to tell of her vocation, how nuns from other congregations wanted her to join their congregation, even going so far as to try their wimples on her. "One of the congregations had the name of the Immaculate," said Bernadette, to which Mother Marie-Thérèse Vauzou, the mistress of novices, primly said, "Our congregation was one of the first to be dedicated to the Immaculate Conception." After relating her story, Bernadette changed from her traveling clothes to the postulants' bonnet and cape, in which habit it would be very difficult to distinguish her from the rest of the postulants.

Homesickness hit her on her first Sunday away from home, so much so that in a letter written to the sisters at the Hospice of Lourdes, she wrote, "I have to tell you that Léontine (her fellow-postulant from Lourdes) and I watered Sunday with our tears. The good sisters encouraged us by saying this was a mark of a good vocation." That was not the only day homesickness gripped her. In the same letter she adds that she often went to visit the statue of "Our Lady of the Waters" at the bottom of the convent garden: "It's there I was able to unburden my heart those first days; and, ever since, our dear mistress has allowed us to go there every day."

Her time spent at the Hospice of Lourdes was counted in her postulancy, because three weeks after her arrival at the motherhouse she became a novice. Before taking the novice's habit, she had to make a retreat with the rest of her class. Father Victor Douce, a Marist, gave the first instruction. He was to be her confessor for eleven of her thirteen years in the convent. Father Claude Raccurt, another Marist, preached the rest of the retreat.

The superiors did not want Bernadette to stand out, but they could do nothing about her size. Ranks were formed according to height, smallest first, and what else could they do but let Bernadette, the smallest sister in the community with her four feet seven inches, lead the way. Sister Emilie Marcillac, who was a trifle taller than she was, was her companion in ranks. Because of their approximate size, Bernadette called her, her twin.

Novice

She was invested in the novice's habit on July 29th and given her new name in religion. Her new name differed little from her baptismal name: Marie-Bernarde; she was now Sister Marie-Bernard, the masculine form of her saint's name, Bernard, the Founder of the Cistercians.

The superiors' fears that the bishop was tempting Providence in having them accept her seemed justified, for she had just begun her novitiate at the end of July, when about August 15th she had to go to the infirmary. On October 25th her condition was so bad, she was anointed. If she was going to die, the superiors wanted her a full member of their congregation. They wanted her to take her vows on her deathbed. The bishop himself came to receive her vows. She could barely breathe. The bishop told her he would pronounce the formula for her; all she had to do was say "Amen." And so it was.

The bishop had just left the convent when Bernadette could talk again, and smilingly told her Superior General, "...I won't die tonight." Annoyed by all the disturbance Bernadette had caused when she knew she was not going to die that night, the Superior General half-jokingly threatened to take back her professional veil and cross if she were still alive the following morning. Playfully called a thief by Sister Charles Ramillon for the sneaky way in which she "stole" her profession cross and veil, she answered, "Call me thief if you will, but these belong to me!" The Superior General never did make good her threat.

On February 2, 1867, Bernadette was well enough to resume her life as a novice. Every novice goes through a testing period, and the prime tester is the mistress of novices. The mistress is in sole command of the novice's life, both internal and external. It is she who judges whether a novice will stay or leave; her judgment rules supreme. The novice does what she is told; and the way she accepts the guidance, reacts to conditions and accomplishes the demands of the mistress are what are used to judge the mettle of the novice. If she reaches the standards set by the mistress, she will become a professed sister, a member of the congregation.

Bernadette's mistress of novices was Mother Marie-Thérèse Vauzou, of upper-middle class stock, and very conscious of her up-bringing. She was forty-one when she met Bernadette; Bernadette was twenty-two. Mother Marie-Thérèse had been mistress of novices for five years, but before becoming mistress she had had a series of successes in a very active religious life, with more signal successes to come. She was to be mistress of novices for twenty years and then to be elected Superior General, with five re-elections to this top office—

Superior General for eighteen years. In Bernadette's novice years, Mother Marie-Thérèse was not only the Mistress of the Novices, but by a strange turn of events, she had pretty much the run of the whole convent. The Superior General, Mother Josephine Imbert, was of a sickly disposition, and, even though she had two Assistants and a Secretary to rely on, she deferred to Mother Marie-Thérèse in almost everything. Because of these conditions, Bernadette was to come under her authority for eleven of her thirteen years of religious life. Only when Mother Josephine resigned and Mother Adelaide Dons was elected Superior General were conditions to change.

Much has been written on the relations between Mother Marie-Thérèse and Bernadette, not much of it in Mother Marie-Thérèse's favor. To be fair, however, it has to be kept in mind that the mistress had a job to do: to form the postulants and novices. The methods of formation in the 1860's and 1870's were strict. They were to be a little more strict with Bernadette, because the superiors had agreed to treat Bernadette coldly in order to keep her humble. Since the mistress had most to do with her, it was up to her to see that the course of action agreed upon would be carried out.

To begin with, before Bernadette's arrival, Mother Marie-Thérèse was thrilled at the thought of having in her care the girl "whose eyes had seen the Blessed Virgin." It was not too long before this thrill disappeared. Three things seemed to have contributed to the change. The first was the matter of Bernadette's secrets, the three she had received from the Lady at the grotto. Postulants and novices were not supposed to have secrets from the Mother Mistress, as far as Mother Mistress was concerned. Bernadette had been told by her Lady to tell no one her secrets, and, to Bernadette, that included the Mistress of Novices. Besides this, in other things, Bernadette could always relate to more simple people and confided in Mother Eléonore Cassagnes and Mother Nathalie Portat, much to the annoyance of Mother Marie-Thérèse. The second reason for the change of attitude on the mistress' part was that she found Bernadette too "touchy." Bernadette was quick of tongue, a trait she had inherited from her Pyrenean forebears, and it was to take a long time for her to learn to hold her tongue. Mother Marie-Thérèse could not equate "touchiness" with "the eyes that had seen the Virgin Mary." The last reason for the change is more subtle. Mother Marie-Thérèse was a bit of a snob. She was quoted as saying, "She was a little country girl. If the Blessed Virgin wanted to appear some place on earth, why would she choose a common country girl without any education instead of a virtuous, educated religious?"

Her doubts concerning Lourdes were to die hard. After all, the Bishop's Commission had said "the apparition was worthy of belief by the faithful"; no one was compelled to believe it. Mother Marie-Thérèse expressed her doubts on several´occasions. Regarding the Dean's demand of the Lady, she told Mother Marie-Thérèse Bordenave, "Just the same, the flower bush never did blossom!" And to an acting chaplain, Father Boillot, she said, "There are bishops who don't believe in it (Lourdes)!" as if to justify her own stand.

As for believing in Bernadette, her doubts were a little more positive. To Mother Marie-Thérèse Bordenave she confided, "I do not understand how the Blessed Virgin could show herself to Bernadette; there are souls much more delicate and trained! But...!" Later still she was to say to Sister Stanislaus Pascal, "Oh! If I could only have my say at Bernadette's canonization!" suggesting she would make an excellent devil's advocate.

Mother Marie-Thérèse Vauzou was Superior General from 1881-1899. During that period there was never any serious question of opening the process for Bernadette's beatification, but after her retirement, her successor, Mother Josephine Forestier, brought the subject up to her and got for an answer, "Wait till I'm dead!" Before she died in 1907, it was her fate to be retired at the Hospice of Lourdes, where she finally gave in to the charm of Lourdes and was heard praying, "Our Lady of Lourdes, help me in my agony." Two months before her death she confessed, "God permitted Mother Josephine Imbert and I to be harsh to Sister Marie-Bernard, to keep her humble."

Most of Bernadette's contemporaries admit the harshness of Mother Mistress but temper it by saying that, in spite of it, she was always fair.

All novices got a good dose of testing. One novice, Sister Julienne Camartin, put it lightly by saying, "I would look in vain to find one floor tile in the novitiate I haven't kissed!" At the time tile-kissing was a usual form of penance, and Bernadette had her share of kissing the floor. Her fellows looked on Bernadette as someone special, so that when she was corrected it made more of an impression on them. One of them, Sister Stéphanie Vareillaud, could not help saying, "I would not have wanted to be in her place!" There is much truth in Bernadette's being picked on with a little more harshness than the rest, because Mother Marie-Thérèse admitted to Mother Léontine Villaret, "Every time I had something to say to Bernadette, I was prompted to say it sharply.... In the novitiate, I had novices before whom I would rather have knelt than before Bernadette."

Bernadette herself was never heard to complain about her treatment; rather, she defended her Mistress' way of treating her, saying she acted thus to put down her pride. Because she saw less of Mother Josephine Imbert, who generally treated her very coldly so as not to show any sign of favoritism, Bernadette's silence was not so closed. She did say, "Mother Josephine, oh! how I fear her!" There may have been fear in Bernadette's attitude to her Mistress of Novices, but if there was she never expressed it openly.

While these new "mothers" were giving Bernadette the treatment they thought they should "to keep her humble," she suffered a loss that hurt much more than that. Her mother, Louise Soubirous, passed away on the feast of the Immaculate Conception, December 8, 1866. Worn out by the hard life she had lived, including giving birth to nine children, she died at forty-one. To Bernadette, who had been very close to her mother, this death affected her very deeply. To the Abbé Pomian, her first confessor at the Hospice of Lourdes, she wrote, "I learned of my mother's death before I even knew she was sick."

Anyone who recovers after taking vows on her deathbed must take vows more solemnly with the other novices at the end of the novitiate year. Bernadette must have passed the tests of her Mistress of Novices, because on October 30, 1867, she took her temporary vows with her class. She was now a Sister of Charity and Christian Education of Nevers.

Newly-Professed

Bernadette's life as a professed sister began on a sour note. She took her vows in the morning of October 30th, 1867—four of them at that time: poverty, chastity, obedience and charity—before Bishop Forcade, the same bishop who had pronounced the formula for her on her deathbed a year before. All was sunshine and light. The sunshine, however, was to cloud up in the afternoon.

Everyone was always asking her for prayers, and on the morning of her profession Marie De-Wint asked her to pray for her perseverance in her vocation. The ceremony over, Bernadette sought her out to tell her, "You will be a religious but not with us." As Bernadette had said Marie DeWint later became Sister Marie de Sainte Magdeleine in the Congregation of the Sisters of God.

It was the custom to give the newly-professed their "destinations" on the same day they took their vows. The bishop presided in the novices' conference room. Forty-three of the newly-professed received their crucifix, their Constitution Book and a letter containing their destination. Everyone in the class went through the ceremony except Bernadette; the bishop seemed to have forgotten her. This bothered her, for she bent toward her neighbor, Sister Anastasia Carriere, and whispered, "Everybody's got something.... I'd like to have something too, like everybody else."

As though as an afterthought, the bishop turned to Mother Josephine Imbert and asked, "What of Sister Marie-Bernard?" "Bishop," said the Mother General, "she's good for nothing." This was said smilingly and only loud enough for those in the immediate chairs to hear, but it was said. In a voice loud enough to be heard by all, the bishop said to Bernadette, "Is it true, Sister Marie-Bernard, that you're good for nothing?" "It's true," said Bernadette. "Then what are we going to do with you?" asked the bishop. Bernadette's quick tongue flashed out, "I told you that at Lourdes when you wanted me to enter the community: you said it wouldn't make any difference!" At this unexpected answer, the Mother General stepped in. "If it is all right with you, Bishop, we could, out of charity, keep her at the mother house and give her some kind of job in the infirmary, like cleaning up or passing out sugar-coated pills. Since she's always sick, this would be just the thing." The bishop nodded, and Bernadette said, "I'll try." In episcopal tones the bishop said, "I assign you to the duty of prayer."

This little game played in front of a large community had been pre-arranged. A "destination" to the mother house was considered a plum, and Bernadette could not be singled out to receive a plum. Besides, the superiors had decided that it was much safer to shelter her in the mother house than to send her to some other house of the Congregation, where the crowds would again be chasing after her. This served two purposes: it kept Bernadette humble and solved a delicate problem for the superiors.

But to Bernadette, being publicly called useless, or more degradingly, "good-for-nothing," coming at a time when she had not gone that far on the road to perfection, was an unexpected humiliation. In the recreation that followed, no one would have guessed how deep the hurt was, but years later she admitted how much it had stung.

Bernadette was just beginning on the long road to mastering herself, and what she was so frequently to counsel others, she was putting into practice herself. One of her first patients in the infirmary was Sister Augustine Brusson, who was suffering from bronchitis and being very disagreeable about her sickness. "Come on, my big Augustine, this is for the good Lord," she told her. "We have to suffer for Him, He suffered so much for us."

Later to Sister Dominique Brunet, suffering from a toothache, she gave her idea on suffering. Sister Dominique was very happy to see Bernadette when she arrived in the infirmary, but not so happy to see the dentist waiting for her. There was no such thing as anesthesia at the time, and when the dentist finished with her, she was very put out with him, "Oh! That man! Did he hurt me!" Bernadette gave her a questioning look and asked, "Miss, don't you want to suffer?" as though saying that if a religious has a chance to suffer, she should never reject the opportunity.

Her whole aim in life, she gave to Sister Vincent Garros, "The longer we drag on earth and attach ourselves to it, the more we lose. We have to work for heaven."

Infirmarian

As the Mother General had promised the bishop on Bernadette's Profession Day, she did name Bernadette Assistant-Infirmarian. The assignment lasted from 1867 till October 1873. When Sister Martha Forest, the infirmarian, could no longer fulfill her office because of illness in 1870, Bernadette became infirmarian in her stead, but minus the title; perhaps as a continuation of the superiors' treatment of not giving Bernadette any opportunity to think she was important. The title made no difference; she surprised everyone by the way she handled the details of her duties. She had all the instincts of an efficient nurse and the personality to go with it.

The main difficulty was her own health. The Mother General had been correct when she said, "...since she is always sick, this (the infirmary job) would be just the thing." During her tenure of office she was in bed at Easter 1869 and back in bed in October. On the 12th of April, 1870 both infirmarians were bed-ridden. She enjoyed a respite from May 5, 1870 till the beginning of 1872, but the winter of that year saw her again a patient. February 3, 1873 saw her very sick and again on April 13th, for fifteen days. Another relapse on June 3rd was so bad that she was anointed for the third time in her then twenty-nine years of life. The convent doctor finally decided that the job was too confining for a person in her condition, and on October 30, 1873, she was relieved of her infirmary duties.

When one hears of the protracted periods of her illnesses, it would appear she did not have much time to act as infirmarian; nothing is further from the truth. She applied herself to learning her job. She made meticulous notes on dosages of medicine for various sicknesses and mastered the metric system. Her notes remain, beginning with equivalents: 1 grain = 5 centigrams; 3 scruples or a gross = 4 grains; 1 ounce = 32 grams, then applying these measures to the patients she attended. She was so good at her duty that in 1872 the convent doctor, Doctor Robert St. Cyr, wrote the following to an inquiry about her: "As an infirmarian she does her job to perfection. Small, delicate-looking, she is twenty-seven years old. Of a calm and tender nature, she tends the sick with much perception, without omitting anything in the given prescriptions; she also wields great influence, and, for my part, I trust her completely."

The sick sisters were happy to be attended by Bernadette, not only for her nursing talents but for her compassion as well. She was always able to find the right words to encourage the sufferer, as, for example, the time she was putting drops in Sister Angela's eyes and said, "How come? I give you one drop and you return many!" She never let her pity spoil her patients.

As in the rest of the convent, silence was to be observed at the proper times, but some patients took advantage of their condition. One "Hush!" or a frowning "Light-headed!" from her to the culprits was enough to bring back order in the infirmary.

She could be stern when she thought it necessary. Feeling perfectly fit one day, Sister Eudoxia Chatelain left the infirmary without being told she could leave. Meeting Bernadette, she was told to go back to bed, with the admonition, "Sacrifice is worth more than prayer!" and was kept in bed till the next day, when she was properly released. Sister Julienne Capmartin, whom Bernadette caught reading her Children of Mary manual when she was supposed to be entirely under the blankets to make her perspire, lost her manual to her nurse, who snappishly told her, "Now, there's fervor born of disobedience!" Bernadette could be wily enough when she was sick herself. One such time, early in the morning, Bernadette had Sister Julie Durand open the windows to cool off. The mistress of novices, Mother Marie-Thérèse, came along and scolded Bernadette about having the windows open, and then left. Sister Julie promptly went to close the windows only to be stopped by Bernadette, who told her, "Mother just scolded me about asking to have the windows open; she said nothing about closing them!"

During this period Bernadette landed in the middle of a fight that was going on outside the convent. Back in Lourdes, Henri Lassérre was writing a book about the apparitions but was not making enough progress to suit the chaplains at the grotto, who began publishing their own popular history of the events that took place there. This infuriated Lassérre, who thought very little of their efforts. He made a special visit to Nevers to see Bernadette and returned to finish off his rivals. To defend his chaplains' "Little History," the superior, Father Sempé, made the trip to Nevers to question Bernadette more closely for ammunition to answer his attacker. This infighting worried Bernadette, who had come to the convent to hide, not to be the center of controversy.

The Franco-Prussian War of 1870 affected the convent in a definite way, since the army took over a part of it. In November of 1870, Bernadette wrote her father that she would just as soon miss seeing the Prussians but that she was not afraid of them. "God is everywhere," she wrote, "even in the midst of the Prussians.... As a little girl, after one of the Curé's sermons, I heard people say, 'Bah! He's only doing his job.' I think the Prussians are only doing their job."

The secrets of Bernadette intrigued the army during this war, when an army officer questioned her. He was the Chevalier Gougenot des Mousseau:

"Have you had at the grotto or since any revelations regarding the future or the destiny of France? Did the Blessed Virgin give you any warnings or threats about France?"

"No."

"The Prussians are at our doors; aren't you just a little bit afraid?"

"No."

"There's nothing to be afraid of, then?"

"I only fear bad Catholics."

"Don't you fear anything else?"

"No, nothing."

Her father's death on March 4, 1871 greatly saddened her. Her father had been very fond of his eldest, and she returned his love. To her cousin Jeanne Védère, she had once said, "It seems to me that I have a preference for my father. I love my mother very much, but I seem drawn to my father. I don't know why, unless it's that my father came to see me daily (at Bartrès) and my mother rarely came." She told Sister Madeleine Bounaix that at the very time she was praying for the dying, without knowing it, she was including her father in her prayers.

Charm

In spite of themselves, the superiors could not help but see that Bernadette was "good medicine," not only for her patients in the infirmary, but especially for the postulants and novices. Professed sisters were not to mix with the postulants and novices, except on special occasions. With Bernadette, they ignored their own rule and allowed her to fraternize, because they knew she raised their spirits. She could come and go freely with them during their recreations, and, even outside that time, the mistress of novices would often bring homesick or troubled novices to her to make them forget their troubles. Even when she was in bed sick, on occasion the mistress would allow her to speak to some about her visions in order to shake them out of their self-pity.

The postulants and novices thought so highly of her that sometimes they would be carried away with their admiration. Then Bernadette would become very annoyed. "Since you give me honors not due to me," she once said, "I won't stay with you during recreation." Sister Clémence Chasan said it took some doing to keep her with them. She agreed to stay only after they promised they would treat her more simply.

As she herself never put on airs, she deflated those who did. Sister Eléonore Bonnet was very proud of her voice and singing. Before some of the sisters one day, she was very embarrassed by Bernadette, who went into gales of laughter, perhaps flattening a few of Sister Eléonore's notes. To her protest some time later, Bernadette answered her, "Yes, I did have a good laugh, but you have to admit there was much to laugh about," driving the point more deeply home.

As often as they could, groups of sisters came to visit her, even early in the morning, when she would have liked to prolong her thanksgiving after receiving Holy Communion. One day she mentioned this to Sister Marcelle Vialle and asked her what she would do to remedy this situation. "If you would allow me," said Sister Marcelle, "I'll apply the remedy," and with that locked the door, so that no one could enter. Coming back in fifteen minutes, she unlocked the door and got thanked by Bernadette for her help. She must have thought it over during the day, for that night she asked Sister Marcelle, "You won't lock me in anymore, will you?" No reasons were given and sister didn't ask why.

Some people make friends easily; others value their privacy more than friendship and are satisfied with having acquaintances, the degree of their familiarity with them varying with each one. Bernadette was chary of giving her friendship to anyone; but once it was given, it was a lasting gift.

Small herself, she loved smallness. As far back as her stay in Bartrès, when she was thirteen, tending the Laguës' sheep, her favorite among the flock was a small, cuddly, white lamb. Though he caused her trouble by tumbling her "month of Mary" altars and butting her at the knees to make her fall, she "punished" him by giving him bread and salt, of which he was most fond. Transferring this preference for smallness to people, she loved children, and, on becoming a religious, loved "the little bonnets" (the postulants).

When it came to individual friends, her childhood saw her with companions rather than friends. She did make a good friend of a first cousin of hers, Jeanne Védère, even though Jeanne was seventeen years her senior. Bernadette arranged it to have Jeanne close to her at the March 4th apparition. Jeanne visited at the "Cachot," and Bernadette spent time with her in Momères, where Jeanne lived and taught class. They often had confidential chats about their respective vocations. Jeanne eventually became a Trappistine nun.

In her teens at the Hospice of Lourdes, she made one lifelong friend, Julie Garros, who, though younger than Bernadette, was more advanced in her studies, causing the Sisters to have her help Bernadette begin the mastery of her ABC's. Far from resenting this, Bernadette became closely attached to Julie. When Bernadette told Julie, Julie was going to be a Sister of Nevers, Julie vehemently objected. She could never see herself walled up in a convent, not this free and easy spirit! When she finally did arrive at Nevers, a few years after Bernadette had entered, Bernadette greeted her with, "Ah! Here you are, you bad subject! You finally gave in!" Bernadette was named her "guardian angel" to orient her to her new way of life. Since the ban on talk of the grotto and the apparitions was not in force during this orientation period, they both covered the subject thoroughly. Julie was such a close friend that she could ask Bernadette with impunity, "What were the three secrets the Blessed Virgin told you at the grotto?" But her boldness got her no further than it got anyone else, because "Bernadette laughed in my face," says Julie, "and said, 'That's my business, not yours!' "

The blithe spirit of Julie felt hemmed in during her first weeks at the convent and wanted its freedom. Lourdes looked so appealing. "Go pray in front of Our Lady of the Novitiate's statue and sleep well," Bernadette told her. The next day Julie changed her mind about leaving. Years later Julie confessed, "She was a mother to me, and I told her all my troubles." Julie's light-headedness got her into many difficulties, giving Bernadette many occasions to correct her. Seeing her make the sign of the cross very skimpily, Bernadette sarcastically asked her, "Have you got a sore arm?" And again on the day Julie was sick in the infirmary and had no napkin to wipe her mouth, she was about to use her handkerchief instead, when Bernadette, tending her, brought her a napkin. "When I would wipe my face at the grotto with my pocket handkerchief," she told Julie, "it was clean!" Julie's quick answer made her smile, "Yes, but it wasn't embroidered!"

During her stay in the infirmary, Bernadette one day brought her some canned fruit. "I'm going to give you a good snack," she told Julie; then to Julie's disappointment, added, "Since it's Saturday we won't eat any. We'll make this sacrifice for the Blessed Virgin." But Julie had a long memory. It was Bernadette's turn to be sick abed, and Julie brought her some burnt chocolate. Tasting the bitter chocolate, she said to Bernadette, "Oh! It's so good! It's delicious!" Bernadette took some and, without batting an eye-lash, said, "You're right! It's much better than usual!"

The day after her profession, Julie was leaving Nevers for her new assignment and asked Bernadette for a souvenir. "When people love each other a lot, there's no need for souvenirs," Bernadette told her, "but, remember, you must love without measure and devote yourself without counting the cost." Julie then gave her a parting kiss and said, "Au Revoir!" to which Bernadette answered, "Not on this earth." That was the last time the two friends saw each other.

Jeanne Jardet was not a sister, but a girl in her early twenties who worked at the convent. After a hot day's work in the kitchen, she went out for air and caught a cold, which put her in bed for two months. Bernadette did not have her in charge, but, out of kindness, visited her often, at the topmost floor of the convent. Winded, she would arrive, tidy Jeanne up and would do the best she could to cheer her up. Thinking she was going to die, Jeanne told her about it, crying her eyes out. "Don't cry," said Bernadette, "God is the Master. You'll see your mother again." Consoled, Jeanne asked her for some Lourdes water, which Bernadette eventually brought her, but in a very tiny bottle. "That's not enough!" said Jeanne, to which Bernadette smilingly answered, "My dear child, quantity doesn't mean anything. Don't take it all at once!" Giving Jeanne a holy picture one day, she told her to recite the prayer on the reverse side every night, and when Jeanne told of this years later, she said, "For sixty years, I haven't missed once!"

During Bernadette's last summer on earth, she spent a very enjoyable afternoon with Sister Victoire Cassou, a distant cousin of hers, just back from Lourdes. They had permission to spend the whole afternoon together. Since Bernadette was able to walk at the time, they began walking up and down the garden, but decided that if the novices saw them together all that time they might be disedified. Bernadette brought Sister Victoire to the convent carriage, where they climbed in and talked away the afternoon on Lourdes and all that was happening in their home town.

Another intimate friend of Bernadette's was Sister Bernard Dalias. They met for the first time on May 16, 1867 and for the last time, two days before Bernadette died. Their first contact came about because Sister Bernard, who had formed her own ideas of Bernadette, could not pick her out among the other sisters and asked Mother Berganot, beside whom she was standing, which nun was Bernadette. "Why, here she is!" said Mother Berganot, pointing to a tiny nun on the other side of her. Like a soap bubble Sister Bernard's conceptions of Bernadette burst, and she could not stop herself from exclaiming, "That!" Extending her little hand, Bernadette, with a beautiful smile on her face, said, "Yes, Miss, it's only that!" And from that moment Bernadette gave her her friendship.

Tending a sick Sister Bernard in the infirmary one day, Bernadette said to her, "You ask for something I wouldn't do for anyone else, but since it's for a Bernard...."

Two days before her death a group of sisters came to the infirmary to see her for the last time. Since her face was turned toward the wall, the sisters could not see her. To get one last look at her, Sister Bernard leaned over at the foot of the bed. Bernadette opened one eye and saw Sister Bernard, whom she signaled to come closer. Bernadette's emaciated little hand feebly clasped Sister Bernard's, and she said, "Adieu... Bernard. This time it's all over." Sister Bernard made a movement to bring Bernadette's hand to her lips, but Bernadette quickly hid her hand under the covers. "Our twelve years of friendship were enclosed in two handclasps," said Sister Bernard. "She hadn't been aware of my companions, which gave me the privilege of a personal, final goodbye," added Sister Bernard.

Most of the sisters who had dealings with Bernadette considered her their friend; but besides her intimate friends, written of already, are a number who were closer to her than others. Among these were: Sister Léontine Mouret, her Lourdes companion, and Sisters Emilie Marcillac, Martha du Rais, Claire Lecocq, Gonzaga Cointe, Marcelline Lannessans and Casimir Callery.

She had a fond affection for Mother Alexandrine Roques, the superior of the Hospice of Lourdes and for Mother Eléonore Cassagnes and Mother Nathalie Portat, members of the administrative staff at Nevers, and for Mother Marie-Bernard Berganot, the superior of Lectoute, whom Bernadette affectionately called her "godmother." She also had a grateful love for Dean Peyramale, once he became her protector, and for Father Sempé, the director of the grotto.

Bernadette was too full of life, even with all her sicknesses, to hide the pleasures she got from her friendships.

Perfectionist

When the Lord preached, "Be you perfect as your Heavenly Father is perfect," He was not saying this for the disciples' benefit alone; He was preaching this for everyone. Religious take this on as a life's work. Bernadette's life as a sister was completely given over to the attempt to comply with the Lord's command; but, as with all others who try, she soon learned that it was not that easy. Forcing her will to conform to the will of the Almighty created problems; Bernadette was so human.

When the superiors named Sister Gabrielle Vigouroux as infirmarian in November 1873, Bernadette was not left without an assignment; she was still part-time infirmarian and part-time sacristan. The second job gave her no trouble, but giving up the reins in the infirmary, where she had been in full charge for three years, to a sister a year younger than she and far less experienced, did not come too easily. Her opinions and practices often clashed with those of the new infirmarian, who quickly learned how to have her own way. All she had to do was to suggest that Bernadette was being self-willed or self-opinionated, and Bernadette swallowed her pride and gave in. At the end of the July retreat, she wrote in her notes: Work at being indifferent. And she did work at it, but it went so much against the grain; she was so spirited and had such an interest in everything that went on around her.

It is possible that Bernadette gave Sister Gabrielle a present she gave to very few, in order to relieve the tensions between them. "While I was nursing her," says Sister Gabrielle, "she gave me an account of the apparitions. I remember her having her eyes fixed on a scene of the grotto of Lourdes, placed at the foot of her bed.... I wrote down what she told me that night or the following morning, in a private, little notebook." The story ended with Bernadette saying, "She (the Blessed Virgin) had blue eyes."

Whether Bernadette got special permission to speak of her visions to Sister Gabrielle from mother mistress or from Mother Josephine Imbert, the Superior General, is not known. Either that is the explanation for her confidences to Sister Gabrielle or the restriction about her talking of the apparitions had been somewhat eased.

Trying to do the right thing caused her difficulties sometimes. Sister Philippine Molinéry tells of a Saturday that Mother Josephine Imbert sent word that Bernadette was not to attend Mass the next day, Sunday. Whether it was the way the message was delivered or what, the following morning came and Bernadette attended Mass in the small tribune near the infirmary. Mother Josephine saw her from the large tribune, and after Mass, standing in the doorway of the infirmary, scolded her soundly for her disobedience and left. After she was gone the only thing a confused Bernadette said, was, "What could I do? I fulfilled the precept!"

To the same Sister Philippine Molinéry, who was a very healthy specimen of a nun, Bernadette said, "How lucky you are, my dear friend! If it were permitted, I would envy you! Ah! If only I could have strong arms like yours, how I would work for the glory of such a Master; but I remain a useless sister, always in bed. Why should I complain? It's God's will, and I must submit to it."

Not very strong, she still kept busy. Sister Valerie Perrinet found her one day painting hearts. "If anyone tells you," she said to her, "that I have no heart, tell them that I make them all day long!"

She would have been a great success in any hospital, because what she told her fellow-sisters, she practiced herself. One of her companions from Lourdes, Sister Vincent Garros, the lively Julie of Hospices days, was sent to the infirmary to learn how to care for the sick. She could not have been blessed with a better teacher. Bernadette knew her trainee. One day Bernadette told her to walk Mother Anne-Marie Lescuse, and added, "You care for her as though she were God Himself!" Sister Vincent protested, "Ah! But there's such a difference!" Bernadette ignored this. "Why," continued Sister Vincent, "doesn't she wear her full habit?" "You come and see her tonight," Bernadette answered her. That night Sister Vincent saw Bernadette treating Mother Anne-Marie's ugly, open sore with so much delicate care that it took her by surprise. The sore repelled Sister Vincent, and she took no pains to hide it. "What a Sister of Charity you'll make. You have no faith!" Bernadette rebuked her. The next day Sister Vincent helped Bernadette tend the ugly sore but made sure she did not come in contact with it.

When Mother Anne-Marie died, June 29, 1874, Bernadette invited Sister Vincent to prepare her body for burial, but Sister Vincent refused; the idea disgusted her. "Coward! you'll never make a Sister of Charity," Bernadette told her. One of the customs of the convent was for each sister to give their deceased sisters a parting kiss. Sister Vincent balked at this but forced herself to kiss Mother Anne-Marie, though much against her will. Bernadette's sarcasm bit deeply: "What's a Sister of Charity who can't touch the dead?"

She knew how to reach Sister Vincent. Besides knowing her at the Hospice in Lourdes, she had coifed her the day she took the habit and had told her that day, "All those I put on, stay!" Before leaving the mother house for a new nursing assignment, Sister Vincent listened to Bernadette tell her, "Don't forget to see our Lord in the person of the poor...the more disgusting the poor person, the more love you must give him." And, "When one tends the sick, one must leave before being thanked. The

honor of caring for the sick is reward enough."
And finally, "Spend yourself in the service of
the poor, but prudently. Don't let yourself be
discouraged. Pour out your love for the Blessed
Virgin." And as if looking into the future,
"When people love each other there is no need
of exchanging gifts. They must love each other
without measure, without counting the cost.
Let us embrace each other for the last time."
They were not to see each other again.

Trying to be indifferent had its price, a price
that Bernadette paid. Reminded by Sister Victorine Poux of her reactions and resentments at
the Hospice of Lourdes years before, her answer
was, "Now I'm indifferent." Fighting her inner
resentments to the way she was often treated
cost her a great deal. Sometimes the superiors
thought they were putting one over on her, but
Bernadette was usually alert to their cunning.
Returning shortly from an errand one day, she
was asked how it was that she was back so
quickly. "Because they're reading something
about Lourdes, they put me out the door," she
blithely answered.

One of the reasons Bishop Forcade had pres-
sured the superiors of Nevers to accept Bernadette was to remove her from Lourdes, where so
many daily callers bothered her greatly. Bishop
Laurence of Tarbes and Dean Peyramale had
agreed with the move, to keep her from being
spoiled. Now that she was at the convent of
Nevers, miles from Lourdes, she should have
been shielded from all callers, but that did not
happen. Her fame had preceded her, and more

people wanted to see her and speak to her. The Bishop of Nevers had made it a rule that only bishops could see her, but he made many exceptions to his own rule, and priests, religious and lay people continued to call. They wearied her, and though she would willingly have renounced all calls, she went to the parlor out of obedience to her superiors' wishes.

Some of her visitors were doubters or disbelievers in Lourdes and tried to prove the falsity of her claims. It was quite a strain on her to try to remain courteous, kind and affable with them. Others were not only believers but ardent admirers of hers, who caused her more pain and misery than the doubters and disbelievers. Since she did not think any praise was due her, she wanted none of it; and when these well-intentioned people insisted on lavishing her with it, it distressed her deeply. All the superlatives one could think of were owed to the Blessed Virgin, as she saw it; but to herself, her continued reply was, "If the Blessed Virgin could have found someone more ignorant than I, she would have chosen her." With Bernadette, this was not something put on; she really believed it.

It is easy to see why Bernadette would have loved to see the visiting bishops stay in their dioceses, when one reads the list of those who came to see her: Bishop Forcade, the bishop of Nevers, visited frequently, oftentimes bringing other bishops along with him; the Apostolic Nuncio, Bishop Chigi; Bishop Dupanloup of Orleans; Bishop de Dreux-Brézé of Moulins;

Bishop de Leseleuc de Kérouara of Autun;
Bishop Bourret of Rodez; Bishop Pichenot of
Tarbes, Bishop Laurence's successor; Bishop de
Ladoue, Bishop Forcade's successor and Bishop
Machebeuf of Colorado, U.S.A. L'Abbé Pomian,
her first confessor in Lourdes visited her twice,
and the chaplains at the convent were very frequent visitors, including L'Abbé Perreau, a sort
of "second chaplain" to the mother house.
Laymen too came in the persons of Henri Las-
sèrre, the historian of the Apparitions, and the
photographer, Provost.

Provost was one person the Mother General
did not want around the mother house; but
back in Lourdes, those building the basilica
needed money, and they knew that Bernadette
was their most precious commodity. Her pictures sold like hot cakes, and the price had gone
up from ten centimes apiece in the early days to
a franc. Once again photographers petitioned
the bishop. Pictures of Bernadette as a nun were
not yet on the market. Provost, a Toulouse photographer, obtained all the necessary permissions and appeared at the convent, not only to
the displeasure of the Mother General but more
so to Bernadette herself. She had come to the
convent to escape all publicity and had practically been promised she would never be bothered again. It cost her terribly to go down to be
photographed. She showed her resentment by
poking her coif while getting ready. Sister Marie
Mespouilhé reminded her that that was not exactly the way to act, to which she agreed and
apologized for her actions. Provost took eight

different poses, and, poor Bernadette, she just could not gear her face to its usual serenity; she appears deathly bored with the whole procedure.

These unending visits were the emery cloth God was using to round out her perfection. Her natural wishes were for anonymity; His seemed those of making sure His Mother's shrine would continue in the public eye, with Bernadette lending all she could to help keep it there.

Her attachment to the grotto was one of the last she gave up. In the beginning when people asked her if she would like to re-visit the grotto, she answered variously: "If I could be a little bird," or "If I could do it in a balloon"; or "I wouldn't choose a pilgrimage day!" After some years the tie was fully broken, and her answers were in the negative: "No, foolish people would leave the Blessed Virgin and follow me"; or "No, I'm more happy here in my bed than a queen on her throne." Her sacrifice was complete the day she told Mother Ursula Lasalle, "My mission is finished at Lourdes. What would I do there?"

Trying to be perfect was her one aim, and whatever it took to keep pushing forward, she continued to spend herself doing it.

Prayer Life

There was nothing showy about Bernadette's private devotions, but since she was
under constant observation, much is known
about them. The one thing that struck everyone
was the way she made the sign of the cross. She
had been taught at the grotto by the Virgin herself and had learned her lesson well. Occasionally she would notice the way people crossed
themselves. Seeing Sister Emilienne Duboé
botch one up one day, she told her, "You have
to pay attention, for it means a great deal to
make the sign of the cross well."

People did notice how deeply recollected
she was in the chapel. In order to shut out
distractions, she would pull the sides of her veil
around her face to make them like a pair of
blinders. Mother mistress of novices observed
this singular way of acting and questioned her
about it. Her reply was, "It's my little house,"
and mother mistress did nothing to stop her. In
her last years while in the infirmary, the tented
canopy over her bed gave her the idea of calling
her bed her "white chapel." Since she could not
attend services in the convent chapel, her
"white chapel" became her place of worship.

A distant relative of hers, Sister Victoire Cassou, downhearted at a change of assignment. stopped over at the mother house at Christmas time in 1871, while awaiting the change. Bernadette was sensitive to the feelings of others and raised her cousin's spirits by telling her, "At Midnight Mass, come next to me; there's room." Sister Victoire relates her experience: "I was very happy at the invitation. I could see for myself how recollected she was. Hidden in her veil, nothing could distract her. After receiving Communion she went into such deep absorption that everyone left the chapel without her noticing them. I stayed glued to the spot, having no desire to go to the refectory with the others. I watched her for a long time without her being conscious of it. Her face was radiant... like during her ecstasies at the apparitions. When sister portress came to lock the doors, she roughly rattled the handle of the door. This brought Bernadette back to reality. She got up and left, with me in her wake.... In the cloister she bent toward me and whispered, 'You didn't have anything to eat.' I answered, 'Neither did you.' " And Sister Victoire concludes, "She retired silently."

Her love of the Holy Eucharist and the agonizing Christ were first in her heart, and though books concerning them interested her, she preferred reading the Gospels than having people explain them.

The new chaplain, Father Febvre, had preached on sin, and to Sister Casimir Callery, whom she called "Seraphim," because she had acted the role of a seraph on mother mistress' feast day, she said, "Oh Seraphim, I'm so happy!"

"About what?" queried sister.

"Didn't you hear the sermon?"

"Sure I did."

"Well, the chaplain said when we don't want to commit sin, we don't sin."

"Yes," answered sister, "I heard that, so what?"

"I never wanted to commit a sin, so I have never committed one!"

Joy radiated her face, reported Sister Casimir who added, "I envied her her happiness, because I couldn't say as much."

Our Lady was her most intimate saint, and who could doubt that? Never could she be forced to say that different statues of the Virgin were pretty. Not to hurt others' feelings, she would say, "It is impossible here on earth to represent her as she is," as she once told Sister Joseph Caldairou. She confessed that statues of the Virgin, far from helping her fervor, detracted from it. Knowing how close she was to the Blessed Virgin, people were forever asking her to pray to her for them. She would accede but never without adding, "You pray for me." She had a low estimate of her worth, and to Sister Aurélie Gouteyron she said, "When I'm dead people will say: 'She saw the Blessed Virgin; she's a saint'; and all the while I'll be grilling in purgatory." With the innumerable requests for her prayers, she solved the problem of praying for them all: every day she said a rosary for all of them and their intentions.

"She seized every chance to show her love for the Blessed Virgin, in speaking of her on her feasts, on the graces she had received and in the confidence we ought to have in her," said Sister Casimir. To Sister Emilienne Duboé she rhapsodized, "If you only knew the beauty I have seen there (at the grotto)" and added, "If you only knew how good the Blessed Virgin is!"

To Sister Vincent Garros, her fellow-townsman, who complained about not being able to meditate, she advised, "Transport yourself to the Garden of Olives or to the foot of the cross and stay there. Our Lord will speak to you, you listen...." Only the mischievous Julie in Sister Vincent could get by with, "I went, but our Lord said nothing to me." She one day asked Bernadette, "How do you stay so long in thanksgiving?" Bernadette answered, "I pretend that the Blessed Virgin has given me the Child Jesus. I hold Him and talk to Him, and He talks to me." Another time she said to her, "When you are in front of the Blessed Sacrament, you have the Blessed Virgin on one side of you to inspire you what to say to our Lord, and on the other side, your guardian angel who jots down your distractions." Another piece of advice to her was, "When you go by the chapel, and haven't the time to stop, tell your guardian angel to take your messages to our Lord in the tabernacle. He'll bring them and then catch up with you." And again, "It's to our advantage to give our Lord a gracious welcome in our hearts, because then He has to pay us rent for lodging Him."

St. Joseph, whom she called her father, was a favorite saint of hers. To Sister Vincent Garros, she gave this tip, "When you can't pray, address yourself to St. Joseph," as if to say he would supply the deficiency. She surprised Sister Marcelline Lannessans one day when sister asked her to petition the Virgin for a favor. She knelt down in front of a statue of St. Joseph and said her prayer. On being told that it was a statue of St. Joseph before whom she prayed to the Virgin, she calmly answered, "There is no jealousy in heaven!"

Her namesake, St. Bernard, was also a familiar of hers, but though she admitted she prayed to him, she didn't care to imitate him. "St. Bernard loved suffering," she told Sister Angela de Filiquier, "but I avoid it as much as I can." She was partial to anyone named Bernard. She called Mother Marie-Bernard Berganot her "godmother," and Sister Bernard Dalias became one of her best friends.

Because long prayers tired her, she was in the habit of saying ejaculatory prayers. To Sister Martha du Rais she confided, "I can't say long prayers, so I make up by saying ejaculatory prayers."

Her Lady at the grotto had given her a cause towards which she could direct her prayers: the conversion of sinners. This was her first intention, though the sick, the dying, the souls in purgatory and other intentions received their share of her prayers. "The souls in purgatory are sure of their salvation, but sinners are in danger," was her way of putting it. "Have you a collection of sinners?" asked Sister Martha du Rais. "Sad to say, there's always a supply," she said. To Sister Michel Gaillard, she counseled, "Every time you go to the chapel, say an act of contrition for them."

The Will of Others

Bernadette grew up doing what others wanted her to do, as her father attests to; but there was another part of her that rebelled. After the apparitions, Dean Peyramale wanted to shelter her in the Hospice, but it took two years to get Bernadette to agree to the separation from her family. The Abbé Pomian had much to do with her training, he being her first confessor. On her entrance in the Hospice, the superiors and the sisters told her what she could do and what she could not do. She had been told that she could freely go to see her family, but that was not always the case, to Bernadette's resentment. Towards the end of her stay at the Hospice, she became a postulant, when she had to curb her will much more than previously. It was in the convent at Nevers where she learned the real cost of obedience. The rule was difficult enough to follow, but add to that the whims and caprices of the superiors and of her fellow-sisters, and Bernadette's troubles can be imagined.

She tasted obedience immediately on her arrival. Her superiors decided that she would give an account of her visions to the assembled sisters on her first day. She would do this in her traveling clothes, to give the recital a bit of Lourdes' flavor; only after, would she change to the postulants' bonnet and cape. She was forbidden to mention the grotto to anyone, except to those allowed by the superiors. The community was forbidden to talk to her about the matter also, a very trying prohibition, since everyone who saw her wanted to question her on the subject.

To add to the difficulty of obedience, the practice of the "culpe" was in full use in the convent in Bernadette's day. A "culpe" is the confession of exterior faults to superiors. On a very cold day, reports Sister Alexis Feral, Bernadette had lit a flaming fire, which had gotten too hot. To cool the room, Bernadette opened the windows during recreation, when along came Mother General, who scolded her roundly, ending with, "Doesn't that bother you?" "Oh! no, my dear Mother," Bernadette sweetly answered. She closed the windows, but having second thoughts about her answer, she later went off to make her culpe.

The sisters who waited on the tables during the meal ate after the rest of the sisters left the refectory, in silence. Bernadette, a waitress one day, put her fork in a platter of carrots but the carrots were so hard that they bounced off her fork and rolled the length of the table, to the merriment of all. After the meal, Bernadette turned to Sister Louise Brusson and said, "Let's go!" Both went off to make their culpe to Mother Mistress, for breaking the silence of the refectory.

In the laundry one day, a very homely postulant kept admiring herself in the reflecting cover of a clothes hamper. When Sister Louise Brusson arrived, Bernadette could stand the vanity of the conceited one no longer. "Put something on that cover," said Bernadette to Sister Louise. Sister took a piece of paper and wrote on it: "Look at your soul!" and glued it on the reflecting surface. Some time later, when Bernadette and Sister Louise were absent, the vain one tried to peek at herself again, but on opening the hamper angrily exclaimed, "Who did this to me?" No one confessed, but they all got a good laugh out of the joke. At the next recreation Bernadette saw Sister Louise and said to her, "Our mistress wants to know the guilty party." Bernadette smiled, admitting her part in the affair. Together they went off to make their culpe.

Sometimes it was a matter of getting permission to do things. In a group one day the sister in charge of the kitchen took a fresh egg out of her apron pocket, and the topic of conversation became eating raw eggs, a feat none of them said they could do. Bernadette said it was easy, and the sister immediately gave her the egg to have her prove it. Bernadette broke the shell and in a jiffy swallowed the contents. "Ah!" she said. "That's it. You make me drink the egg and now I have to go find mother assistant to ask her permission to drink it!" And away she went to find the mother assistant.

On her first sickness in the infirmary, Sister Emilie Marcillac chose Sister Alexandrine (Léontine Mouret, her companion from Lourdes) to assist her in tending Bernadette, a very pleasing choice to Bernadette, who was fond of Léontine; but mother mistress, discovering the reason for Sister Emilie's choice, forbade her to have Léontine in the infirmary. Noticing Léontine's absence, Bernadette asked if she was sick, to which Sister Emilie explained mother mistress' prohibition. "Ah! I understand," was all Bernadette said.

A new reason for her distaste for important people was added to her burden: answering their letters. They wrote to her so as to get a personal answer from her. To Sister Brigitte Hostin, she confessed, "If it were not because of obedience, I wouldn't answer."

Her main cross continued to be visitors. Although her superiors tried to sift them, many slipped through. Bishop Forcade, the bishop of Nevers, gave all his fellow-bishops the freedom to visit her anytime. Bernadette admitted to Sister Joseph Caldairou one day, "I have to go to the parlor. If you only knew how much it cost me! Especially when it is for bishops!"

Her superiors sometimes used strategy so as to hide from her the main reason for the bishops' visits. The Bishop of Rodez wanted to meet her. The superiors got him to give the sisters a conference, after which he was introduced to groups of sisters from different parts of France,

singling out certain sisters as they were presented to kiss the bishop's ring. Bernadette saw
through this and told her cousin, Sister Victoire
Cassou, next to her, "I know what I'll do," and
with that she escaped through a little door near
them; but not before her cousin said, "What
about the indulgence of forty days?" (for kissing
the bishop's ring). "My Jesus, mercy!" said Bernadette, "There's three hundred days!" She only escaped for the moment, for that bishop got a
private interview with her later.

During a period of fair health, she went on a
picnic to Coulanges, where next to the river,
under shady trees the sisters were enjoying
themselves. Someone from the mother house
came and told them they would have to return
quickly because bishops had arrived and were
awaiting them. It was Bernadette they wanted
to see. Very displeased at the abrupt end of their
picnic, Bernadette in a mutinous mood said,
"These good bishops would do better to stay in
their dioceses than to come to see us; we were
so happy here!"

Bishops could be as trying as others who
wanted her to touch things belonging to them.
The bishop of Autun visited her in the infirmary, where she was sick abed. He purposely
let his red skull-cap fall on the bed so that she
would have to return it to him, thus touching it;
but she made no move to pick it up. "Would
you give me back my skull-cap, please, Sister?"
said the bishop. Bernadette ungraciously answered, "Bishop, I did not ask you for it, you

can pick it up yourself." The mother assistant, Mother Louise Ferrand, present at the interview, resolved the impasse by laughingly telling Bernadette, "Come, my dear Sister, return the skull-cap to the Bishop." Only obedience to a superior gained the bishop his wish.

These parlor visits were the one thing that made her rebellious. Being very alert as to what was going on about her, when she guessed they were looking for her to go see visitors, "she would travel the convent from top to bottom and from bottom to top, taking different stairways to escape from being found," as Sister Joseph Garnier put it, "but once she had received the order, she would resign herself and go, often with bad grace." The Mother General reprimanded her for this way of acting, and, though she would promise to amend her ways, it was often too much for her. She felt that she had been promised to be free of these visits once she entered the convent, but the promise wasn't being kept.

On occasion she escaped these ordeals as on the day one of the sister's cousins wanted to see her. The sister went to get permission from the Reverend Mother, who said, since there was no particular reason for the visit, Bernadette could go, but she would leave her free to go or not. The sister went to Bernadette and told her the Reverend Mother had given her permission to go to the parlor. Bernadette wisely asked, "Is that all she said?"

"Well," the sister replied, "she gives you permission to go but leaves you free."

"Oh!" said Bernadette, "she leaves me free, then it's no! no! no!" and with that ran outdoors to the bottom of the convent garden.

Told one day that the Bishop (of Nevers) had come to see her, her answer was, "No, he didn't come to see me but to have me seen!" She had caught sight of him bringing along another bishop.

She resented being gawked at like some freak animal, as she herself called it, and as often as she could avoid it, she would.

When people who did not know her, asked her to see Bernadette, she would say, "I'll go get her," and would disappear, not to return.

Bernadette was a very private person. She understood that, at the time of the apparitions, she was forced to become public property, because the Blessed Virgin wanted to use her to begin great things. For eight years after the apparitions, she had been at the beck and call of anyone who wanted to question her, from the Bishop's Commission to every inquisitive person who came along. At the Hospice of Lourdes, where they had told her they would protect her from all the curious, she had begun to resent these parlor calls, because the promised protection was not forthcoming. She had escaped to Nevers specifically to disappear. Mother Eléonore Cassagnes and others quoted her as saying, "I have come to the convent to hide." To her way of thinking, she was a broom that, once used, is put behind the door till it is needed again. She expressed this very idea to Sister Philippine Molinéry. Now, she was no longer needed, and most of the visitors just wanted to see a spectacle, herself; and she did not want to be a spectacle. Few people have tried so hard to remain hidden as Bernadette tried, yet less than a few people have had to face the ordeal of so much unwanted publicity so constantly.

Even on her sickbed, she had to put up with the daily visits of her fellow sisters. The convent housed two or three hundred nuns, who all wanted to see her, besides the many visiting nuns from other convents, coming to the mother house for one reason or other. Her sicknesses finally carried her off, but the debilitating, daily chore of fighting to remain plain Bernadette Soubirous wore away her energy and caused the sicknesses to produce their inevitable results.

Doing the bidding of others was a hard cross, but it must have been quite a pleasant change to give orders to others from time to time, as in the case of Sister Marcelline Durand. This sister had eye trouble, and the doctors recommended snuff as a cure, but sister was afraid to become addicted and did not want to start. Bernadette, who took snuff by order of the doctor, offered sister her snuff-box, but sister refused to take a pinch. "Take some. That's an order!" insisted Bernadette.

Bernadette Soubirous

(From an oil painting.)

**Jean-Marie
Soubirous**

(Bernadette's brother and sister.)

Marie Soubirous

Photograph of Bernadette.

The Soubirous Family.

The Soubirous
Mill.

The paternal
home of
Bernadette.

The interior of the Soubirous home.

The village of Bartrès.

Bernadette's farmhouse.

Bartrès—The house of Laguës,
where Bernadette lived.

Bartrès—The interior of the residence.

The Apparition. *(Painting at Rome.)*

The Grotto in 1858.

Bernadette
in the costume
of the village.

Don Peyramale,
Pastor at Lourdes.

The Basilica and the Grotto.

First procession—1864.

Bernadette,
now
Sister Marie-
Bernard.

Tomb of Bernadette.
Mother House of the Sisters of Charity
of Nevers.

The Holy Cross infirmary where Bernadette died. *(Her bed is designated by the cross.)*

The tomb of Bernadette.

The tomb of the Saint.

Chapel and tomb of the Saint.

Lourdes in 1877.

Self-Improvement

The notion that Bernadette was always a backward student is not a true one. In her childhood she had attended few classes, both because she was sickly and because of her parents' work hours. She was the eldest and had to stay home to babysit her little brothers. After the apparitions, the Tardhivail sisters took it upon themselves to begin teaching her. Her education got a new impetus when she entered the Hospice of Lourdes. The Tardhivail sisters resented her entrance there, because she would no longer be in their charge; but it was much better for Bernadette, since now she could go to classes on a regular basis. In spite of the many interruptions by the daily visitors, she began to read and write in French. The Bigourdan dialect was all she knew at the time of the apparitions, and the Blessed Virgin had spoken to her in that language.

Her education continued in the convent, where arithmetic ever remained a mystery she unsuccessfully wrestled with and where penmanship was a labored bore. There was a vast improvement, however, in her penmanship from the days when, asked for an autograph, she wrote on the back of holy pictures, "p.p. Bernadette" (*priez pour Bernadette*—pray for Bernadette) to the letters she eventually wrote to her family and friends. In the beginning she had models to follow, but she graduated from that to writing a fair hand. In answering letters to important people, she had her letters corrected before she sent them, because her spelling remained poor. In the Hospice of Lourdes she had told Sister Isabelle Laverchére when asked to conjugate a verb, "My dear Sister, I can't do a verb." In the convent she showed a knack in catching the idiom of the French language, for from knowing no French at all, at the time of the apparitions to the point she was at the end of her life, there was a tremendous progress.

Conscientious about responsibilities, her note in her infirmary book, after enumerating dosages of medicine for the sick, is very enlightening: "Since a change in the position of the comma can bring about a big difference, it's desirable that in formulas, the quantity in grams, decigrams, centigrams and milligrams should be written out in letters (rather than in numbers)."

The results of her education reached a high in a letter she wrote to the Pope, Pius IX. That came about when Bishop de Ladoue, the Bishop of Nevers, before leaving for Rome, wanted her to write to His Holiness, a letter which he would personally deliver. He visited her in the infirmary, where she was sick abed, and told her that the best way of getting a papal blessing was to write to the Pope. Bernadette made the effort, since she thought having a papal blessing a wonderful gift. Sister Gabrielle de Vigouroux, her successor as infirmarian, held the writing board on Bernadette's knees while Bernadette wrote the first draft. Her superiors thought this too simple and revised it a few times before the final draft was given to the bishop to take along with him. Herewith is the first draft, which is Bernadette all over:

Most Holy Father:
I would never have dared to take pen in hand to write to Your Holiness, I a poor, little sister, if Bishop de Ladoue, our worthy bishop, had not encouraged me by telling me that the surest way to receive a blessing from the Holy Father was to write to you, and he would have the kindness to deliver my letter. There was a struggle between my fear and my confidence, poor ignorant me, a little, sick sister: to dare to write to the Holy Father—never! But then, why fear so much, he is my Father, since he represents God on earth—the Holy Triune God, whom I dare receive so often in my poor heart. It's because I'm so weak that I dare receive the God of strength. The same motive encourages me, most Holy Father, to come and throw myself on my knees at your feet, to ask you for your apostolic blessing, which will be, I am sure, a new spurt of strength to my weak soul.

What can I do, most Holy Father, to prove my gratitude? I have been one of your Papal Zouaves for a long time, though unworthy; my weapons are prayer and sacrifice, which I will keep using till my last breath. There only will the weapon of sacrifice fall but that of prayer will accompany me to heaven, where it will be more powerful than in this land of exile. I pray to the Sacred Heart of Jesus and to the Immaculate Heart of Mary to keep you in our midst for a long time, because you make them known and loved so well. It seems to me that every time I pray for your intentions that from heaven the Blessed Virgin must often cast her eyes on you, most Holy Father, because it was you who proclaimed her Immaculate, and that four years later, I did not know what the word meant. I never heard the word before. Since then, on thinking it over, I told myself that the Blessed Virgin is good—it would appear that she came to confirm the word of our Holy Father.

On his return, June 14, 1877, Bishop de Ladoue delivered the Pope's apostolic blessing; it was addressed to Bernadette and to her religious community. His Holiness also sent Bernadette a personal gift, a small silver crucifix.

In the early days of her stay in the convent, before Bernadette took up her infirmary duties, the superiors sent her to help the procurator, Sister Valentine Gleyrose, answer letters; but writing letters bored her to death. They then gave her some filing to do, but this occupation did not last very long.

During some of her free time as infirmarian she sewed. She was adept with the needle, because they gave her all the worst garments to mend. She was aware of this, but she was not conscious of being used for her mending skill. One day a lady of society in Nevers came to the convent with a blanket she was making. Her little boy was sick, and she wanted Bernadette to work on the blanket so that, once repaired by Bernadette, it could cover the little boy, who, the lady believed, would get well, if Bernadette could be gotten to do this. The superiors agreed to have Bernadette do what was asked, but they did not want her to take any self-satisfaction out of it. Ingenuity had to be used so as not to let her know what was going on. Bringing the blanket to the infirmary, Sister Victoire told the sisters there, "Mrs. X has brought this blanket to us. She has, I think, botched up the work and wants us to correct it." With her usual quickness, Bernadette said pleasantly, "Isn't that convenient! These fine ladies mess up their work and want us to repair the damage. Anyway, give it to me and I'll try to fix it." Everything turned out to perfection, because, later, the boy was covered with the finished blanket and recovered his health.

Though her improvement was obvious to everyone, she never looked for compliments, and when they were given, she made little of them. Sister Eléonore Bonnet found her embroidering an alb for Bishop Forcade, newly-named archbishop of Aix, and raved about its fine workmanship. "Oh, Sister!" typically answered Bernadette, "You think it a grand accomplishment to work with needles! Anyone could do as much!"

Family

To Bernadette, family meant a great deal. Her entrance in the Hospice of Lourdes was postponed two years because of family ties. Her father and mother were as opposed to the move as Bernadette was. Since she had been a little mother to her younger sister and her two little brothers, the separation caused her real pain. She had become very fond of her godchild, her brother Bernard-Pierre, born the year before she entered the Hospice. She was close to her three aunts, her mother's sisters, Bernarde, her godmother, Basile and Lucile, and a strong bond existed between her and her cousin Jeanne Védère. She lavished her affection on her second godchild, Bernadette Nicolau, the last of her Aunt Bernarde's children, who was born in 1863, while Bernadette was living at the Hospice.

The relationship between Bernadette and her cousin Jeanne Védère was an interesting one. Jeanne was the daughter of her father's oldest sister, Thècle, and the sister of Bernadette's godfather. Though Bernadette had seen Jean-Marie Vedère, her soldier godfather, only once on one of his rare visits, during which he was wearing the medal of the Legion of Honor, won at Solferino in 1859, she liked him very much. He died in 1864, at which time Bernadette was quoted as saying, "I knew he wouldn't last long. I was told not to attach myself to him so much." But it was Jeanne who enjoyed the most intimate connection with Bernadette, a union not reached by any other person. Although there was a seventeen year difference in their ages, they got along famously, and many of Bernadette's confidences were given to no other.

It was to Jeanne alone that Bernadette revealed the harsh treatment she often got from her foster-mother, Marie Laguës. Though Marie Laguës could be warm at times, she often showed the bad side of her nature. Her brother, l'Abbé Aravant, rebuked her for her shabby treatment of Bernadette, who confided to Jeanne, "She would change her ways for a while but was soon back to her old ways." To everyone else Bernadette had only high praise for her foster-mother.

On the busiest of days at the grotto, March 4th, the day 20,000 congregated, expecting wonders, it was Jeanne to whom Bernadette promised a place next to her. Lost in the huge gathering, Jeanne resigned herself to watching from afar, but Bernadette, true to her word, got the Superintendent of Police and a gendarme to conduct Jeanne next to her. When the vision was over Bernadette told Jeanne, "If you had extended your hand just a bit, you would have touched her (the Lady)."

In the summer of 1858, it was Jeanne who learned that the barricades were not to last. "Will they fall?" asked Jeanne.

"No," answered Bernadette, "those who had them put up will have them removed."

Jeanne learned of Bernadette's disappointment at not being able to attend the ceremonies of installing Fabisch's new statue at the grotto, April 4, 1864. "I am as happy to stay in bed than if I could go to the grotto...I wanted to go see, but God did not want me to. May His will be done. Don't feel sorry for me; when we do God's will, we are not to be pitied," she told Jeanne. (Years later Bernadette was to have a good laugh at the Dean, who was against her being present that day and who could not go himself, because he was too sick to go. To Sister Vincent Garros, she said, "Yes, [I didn't go] but the Blessed Virgin took care of him! She sent him a good colic that prevented him from attending too!")

In 1860-61 Jeanne wanted to enter the convent, but her parents opposed it. "Have you thought of me?" questioned Jeanne. After a moment's reflection, Bernadette answered, "Yes, you'll have to have patience, but you'll succeed." It was then that Jeanne unfolded her plan to enter Carmel. Her father was so opposed to this that she planned to enter the Daughters of Charity, then later transfer to Carmel. "Oh! Never do that!" said Bernadette, "it's better to stay home. It's as though you have the idea of deceiving people and of deceiving God too. You can't deceive God. He is the one giving you the attraction for the cloister, but it is not He who is inspiring you to enter the Sisters of St. Vincent de Paul with the intention of leaving later. You can believe this, God sees your difficulties and allows them. He'll smooth the way when the time comes." After this, Bernadette told Jeanne of her own aspirations to enter the convent.

It was with Jeanne and her family that Bernadette had her longest vacation. Jeanne was a schoolteacher at Momères, and wanted Bernadette to come and stay over for a few days. Momères was also the Dean's hometown, where his brother was a doctor. He gave his permission for Bernadette to go with Jeanne and to stay as long as she wanted to. The stay lasted seven weeks during which Bernadette made up a daily rule for herself to follow and enjoyed the rest. Her cousin Jeanne took her to school a few times, where she loved being with the children; but too many curious people found out she was there and pestered her. Jeanne decided it was best to leave her at home. While vacationing, Bernadette had to go through another session of picture-taking, because Dufour, the photographer, obtained all permissions from the bishop for the session.

On November 21, 1866, a few months after Bernadette had left for Nevers, Jeanne finally became a Trappistine and was called Sister Marie-Gertrude. An irregular correspondence followed, till Bernadette's death, a correspondence in which both could always open their

hearts to each other. Jeanne outlived Bernadette by twenty years; she died in 1899.

Far from Lourdes, Bernadette at Nevers
stayed in touch with her family. With the death
of her mother and father, she took over the task
of eldest daughter. Recalling the decision-
making power of the eldest daughter in the
Lourdes region, a power respected by the rest of
the family, do not think that distance would
diminish Bernadette's influence. She took her
duties as eldest daughter very seriously. News
reached her that made her fret. She had high
hopes that one of her brothers would become a
priest, but though one studied with the Garai-
son Fathers, when it was time for his military
service he joined the army and never resumed
his studies. When her other brother was giving up his studies with the Brothers, and she
learned that her brother-in-law, Toinette's husband, had ideas of having him work in a new
religious-goods store he wanted to open in
Lourdes, she vehemently opposed the idea.
This religious goods store smacked too much of
making money on Bernadette's Lourdes' fame.
When she could not do much about it, she
pleaded with Toinette not to stay open on Sun-
days, as others did. Her main wish for her relatives was that they earn a living but that they
never get rich. Rumors, blown far out of pro-
portion, reached her that caused her useless
worry, but she did worry. Misunderstandings
in the family sent speedy letters to have them
cleared up; she wanted perfect peace among
her own.

Her brother Jean-Marie came to visit her once, as did her sister Toinette with her husband; but their visits were not of the happiest, because Bernadette's health at the time was very poor, putting a pall on the reunions.

She remained ever grateful to anyone who befriended her relatives and wrote letters to them expressing her thanks; to the Bishop of Tarbes, Bishop Laurence; to Dean Peyramale; to Father Sempé, the director of the Grotto Fathers.

Deaths saddened her during her convent days. One joy she got from the news of her mother's death, just five months after her arrival in Nevers, was that it had occurred on December 8th, the feast of the Immaculate Conception; knowing by that, that the Blessed Virgin had taken care of her mother. Her father's death affected her deeply, and her sympathy went out to her sister Toinette, who lost five babies in a row. Her Aunt Lucile's death was another sad blow. She wept copiously at the news of the death of Dean Peyramale. "He accomplished what I couldn't do!" was her sobbing praise of him.

The miles that separated her from her loved ones could not blot them out of her mind. They were frequently in her prayers. She had made it a practice to pray for the dying and was consoled by the fact that she had been praying for the dying at the very time her father was dying.

With the distance between Nevers and Lourdes, the obvious way of keeping in touch with her family was by mail. She wrote quite a number of letters to them when her health permitted, but there were long stretches when letters would remain unanswered. When she heard that her letters were being passed around, it annoyed her. She had always been a private person and wanted the news she sent to remain with the people she wrote to. This slowed down the correspondence too; if they passed out her letters like souvenirs, they would not have many souvenirs to pass out, because she would not write any more.

Possessions

Ownership was something alien to Bernadette. Even the little she had, she gave away. Her mother tried to feed her with white bread when she could, because the usual corn-like bread the family ate disagreed with Bernadette. Her brothers and sisters would snatch this away from her at times, but she made little struggle to keep it. Her visions made her a very popular person, upon whom people wanted to shower their gifts, but she refused them all and insisted that her family do the same. She wanted nothing and would accept nothing from anyone. This disinterestedness amazed everyone, seeing that she and her family were so poor.

If there was one thing she clung to, it was her rosary beads, but the same pair was not her companion for long. She had a cheap pair in her pocket the day of the first apparition and used them regularly, until the day Pauline Sans, a sick woman who could not get to the grotto, gave her hers to carry there. During one apparition, Bernadette began to say the beads using Pauline Sans', much to the Lady's displeasure. Bernadette pocketed Pauline's and used her own from that day on. These beads disappeared, and it was only years later that Bernadette had something to say about them.

The Abbé Junqua, who had been one of her early questioners, claimed he had the beads she prayed with at the grotto. Her answer to that was, "If someone says he has my beads, he stole them; because I never wanted to give them to anyone." A number of people tried exchanging their costly ones for hers, but she always refused. Throughout her life her rosary beads had a way of disappearing. In the convent, years later, Sister Marie Mespouilhé found her rosary in her infirmary bed and put them in her own pocket. Meeting her during the day, Bernadette said to her, "Little Sister, I lost my beads, did you happen to find them? It's funny but rosaries don't stay long in my pocket." Sister Marie gave them back to her, admitting her desire to keep them. "I can't let you have them," said Bernadette. "It's my dear Sister Assistant who gave them to me. When you leave I will give you a small souvenir." She later gave her a small holy picture.

Nothing stayed with her very long; she gave everything away. On leaving the Hospice for the convent, the only two books she had, found their way into the hands of two sisters of the community.

New clothing was not important to her; hand-me-downs suited her as well, provided they were clean. Everyone noticed her neatness. "Patching is our business," Sister Marcelline Lannessans quotes her as saying to the sisters in the sewing room.

After her deathbed profession, she clung to the professional veil and cross all professed sisters receive, but having them did not mean possession. They represented the fact that, once professed, she could not be sent back home because of ill health. After she received Holy Communion in the infirmary, she would deposit her veil on her bed and a novice would fold it up and put it away. Seeing a novice, Sister Rosalie Pérasse, misfold her veil one day, she called her to task. "Come here, I'll show you how. You must learn to fold a veil correctly, since you will soon receive your own," and proceeded to give her a lesson in the care of veils. Her one-time tutor at the Hospice, Julie Garros, now Sister Vincent Garros, was frequently the target of her lectures. Sister Vincent assisted at a celebration of Corpus Christi at the Hospital of Nevers, where the procession wended its way through the garden. Since looking through a veil is most unsatisfactory, Sister Vincent made a hole in her veil with a big pin, the hole large enough to be able to see what was happening. Bernadette heard about this and was indignant. "You have lacked respect for the Blessed Sacrament; you have lacked the spirit of faith; you have disedified your fellow-sisters and also sinned against poverty," she told Sister Vincent. Letting all the other accusations pass, Sister Vincent asked, "How could I sin against poverty?" "In making a hole in your veil," said Bernadette, and so that Sister Vincent would not forget the main reason for her disapproval, she added, "From now on be more respectful of the Blessed Sacrament."

Someone had given her a popular hymnal then being used at the grotto in Lourdes, but she gave it to Sister Bernard Dalias, saying, "Here, take this; it's more your affair than mine. I have permission to get rid of it."

Sister Angela Lompech reports her fight against waste with the novices, "Don't let the water run for nothing," she cautioned them.

Sensing her end approach, she gave away the pictures she had, including those pinned to the drapes on her bed.

Prophecy?

How Bernadette knew certain things before they ever happened is a question not easy to answer. Since she lived in a convent thirteen years of her life, it is not too surprising that many of her "predictions" dealt with vocations to the religious life. Some dealt with vocations to the Sisters of Nevers, but others had to do with vocations to other Congregations.

In the Hospice of Lourdes she had already told Julie Garros that she would be a Sister of Nevers, and in spite of Julie's vehement protestations, she did become one. In her novitiate class Sister Marcelline Lannessans was sick in the infirmary. "You won't fully recover from your sickness," Bernadette told her, "but you won't die from it. You will have to suffer; you will have to work to earn your heaven." Sister Marcelline remained sickly all her life but lived as a nun for forty-five years. To Sister Martha du Rais, whose father strenuously objected to her becoming a nun and threatened to have her taken from the convent, Bernadette said, "You will be a nun in spite of all the opposition." She also told her that all the trouble she was experiencing was a way of buying her vocation. Sister Martha became a nun. To Marie Cointe, a sick postulant, whose older sister had died young, a professed nun of twenty-one, and whom the superiors were sending home, "Don't worry," Bernadette told her, "you'll be back. You'll be a Sister of Nevers." She returned in 1875 and died a nun in 1925, fifty years later. To Marcelline Durand, who had eye trouble for seven months and worried about being sent home, she said, "Rest assured, you'll get well and be admitted to the community." She did recover and did become a sister.

Sister Claire Salvy had pulled a bone and was told by one of the older sisters that she would never be able to become a nun. In the infirmary, Bernadette found out the reason for her sadness and said to her, "Since you want to do the will of God, you'll be a Sister of Nevers. Don't be sad, but you'll have to learn to bear little crosses." She did become a nun.

At other times she told postulants and novices that they would not become Sisters of Nevers but would join other Congregations. To Annette Basset, sick in the infirmary, Bernadette said, "Don't cry. God wants you to be a nun; you will be, but in another Congregation. You have many years to live." Sister Annette recovered her health and lived fifty-eight years as Sister Bertilie with the Sisters of Cluny. On Bernadette's own profession day, Marie de Wint asked her for prayers for perseverance in her vocation. After the ceremony of profession, Bernadette saw her again and told her, "You will be a religious but not with us." Marie became Sister Marie de Sainte Magdeleine with the Sisters of the Mother of God. To Mother Eulalie, worrying about Agnes Martin, a student of hers at Varennes, who was leaving school to go home, and who, Mother Eulalie thought, had a vocation to the sisterhood: "Don't worry. Your Agnes will remain wise." Agnes later joined the Bon Secours Sisters.

Her "predictions" were not restricted to nuns. To Sister Eudoxia Chatelain's brother, Bernadette told him he would become a priest, and, furthermore, he would one day preach in the pulpit of the Convent of Nevers. He did become a priest and fifty-three years later preached a triduum in the Convent of Nevers.

Sister Stanislaus Ducher had been stationed in Sens and badly wanted to return there after her profession, but was told by Mother Louise Ferrand, an Assistant General, that she would not return. Sister Stanislaus told this to Bernadette and Bernadette answered, "You will go back." Sister Stanislaus asked her how that could be, but only got for an answer, "You will go back." When the bishop gave the "obediences" out, he asked Sister Stanislaus, "Where were you?" "At Sens," she answered. "Very well, my daughter," the bishop said. "We are sending you back to Sens."

Despairing of not finding water to supply the Hotel-Dieu in Villefranche, Sister Eugenie Genty told Bernadette how they had spent much money on people hired to find a water supply. Bernadette told her, "Don't worry, my good Mother, you will find water." Later, water was found.

In 1871 Bernadette told Sister Vincent Garros, the same Julie Garros, who said she would never go to the convent, about Father Peyramale, their former pastor in Lourdes, who was then building a new parish church. "He will begin his new church but will never see it finished. He will have built his last home." "Why won't he?" asked Sister Vincent. "Because the next two successors of Bishop Laurence (the Bishop of Tarbes) will oppose it; but they won't last long. The third successor will give his permission, accept the conditions agreed upon and even give a donation for it. Father Peyramale will have to fight, but the Blessed Virgin will protect and help him." As Bernadette predicted, Bishop Pichenot, Bishop Laurence's immediate successor, opposed the project, but was Bishop of Tarbes only from 1870 to 1873, then was made Archbishop of Chambery; Bishop Langenieux, his successor, also opposed the project but was Bishop of Tarbes only from 1873 to 1874, when he was made Archbishop of Rheims. Father Peyramale was able to continue to build under Bishop Jourdan, Bishop Langenieux' successor, but never completed his church; and at his death was buried in the basement of the uncompleted church.

When it came to death and to the dying, Bernadette proved correct again. Concerning her own death, though everyone thought she would die in any one of her asthma attacks, she often told the sisters, "Don't worry, I won't die this time," and continued to live. On one such occasion, Sister Eudoxia Chatelain tells of a group of novices, visiting her shortly after she was anointed June 3, 1873. One robust novice asked her whether she was afraid of dying. She answered that she was not. The novice said, "Your choking attacks are so bad, one of them could carry you off." "You'll die before I do," said Bernadette. The robust one caught pneumonia a few months later and died.

When Sister Vincent Garros asked her what she thought of the new Bishop of Nevers, Bishop de Ladoue, who arrived in 1873, her answer was, "He's small, cold, and he won't last long." He died July 23, 1877.

When Sister Angela Lompech's mother was dying after the birth of her ninth child, Sister Angela thought she would have to leave the convent to go to help her father, because she was the eldest of his children. She told Bernadette of her misfortune, and Bernadette answered her, "Don't cry, the Blessed Virgin will cure her." Sister Angela's mother recovered and lived thirty-eight years after her recovery.

Sister Joseph Ducourt's father quit the practice of his religion, because his daughter entered the convent. On telling Bernadette of her sadness on this account, Bernadette answered her by saying, "Don't worry. Without doubt you won't see your father again, but he'll die holily." Twenty-five years later Sister Joseph's father died a holy death, as the pastor of the parish in which he died testified to Sister Joseph.

Sister Madeleine Pechauzet's mother feared her brother would die in the War of 1870. "Pray hard," said Bernadette, "and you can tell your mother, your brother won't die." He was still alive in 1908.

Sister Julie Heu's blood-sister was dying of typhus. For four days she could not see, hear, or speak. She had received Extreme Unction, and the doctors were waiting for her to die. Sister Julie asked Bernadette to pray for her sister. Later Sister Julie's sister recovered, at the very time Bernadette was praying for her. When Sister Julie went to seek Bernadette to thank her for her prayers, Bernadette hid from her to avoid her thanks.

And lastly, to Sister Vincent Garros, her fellow-sister from Lourdes, who told her one day, "They say you'll return to Lourdes," she answered, "No, never! After my death they'll try to get my miserable carcass, but they won't succeed." As she had predicted, there was an attempt to have her body returned to Lourdes, but it is now one hundred years since her death, April 16, 1879, and her body is preserved and can be seen by anyone who visits the Convent of Nevers, in her shrine in the main chapel of the convent.

Some of these "predictions" could be called "educated guesses" perhaps, but there are some that defy that explanation.

Modesty

For a person who had been the recipient of such favors as Bernadette was given, she took no pride because of it. On a number of occasions she admitted she did not deserve what happened to her at the grotto. "If the Blessed Virgin could have found someone more ignorant than I, she would have chosen her," was the way she summed it up. To Sister Philippine Molinéry she explained her role: "I served the Blessed Virgin like a broom. When she had no further use for me, she put me in my place behind the door."

Those in charge of her were fearful that all the fuss made over her would make her a very proud and conceited girl. The opposite happened: she was a very humble and retiring girl with a very low opinion of herself. She never could understand why people paid her so much attention, and when the crowds carried their admiration too far, she bristled, "How stupid of them!" she would say. When her fellow-novices pitied her for the way the mistress sometimes treated her, she defended the mistress: "Oh! no, the mistress is right, because I'm very proud; but now that I'm here I'll work to correct

myself. It's not like at Lourdes, where I was sur-
rounded by too many people." Her reactions to
the mistress, Mother Thérèse Vauzous, were
simple and childlike. Sister Stanislaus Pascal
tells of the return of the mistress after a few
days' absence. A number of novices waited to
welcome her in the cloister, and on her appearance Bernadette flung herself in her arms
and gave her a big hug. Later Sister Mélanie
Monéry remarked to her, "Sister Marie-Bernard, that was quite a reaction at seeing your
mistress again!" "Yes," said Bernadette, "it was
all too human; I have been very sorry for it."
The mistress belittled her often enough. During
a reading about an apparition of the Blessed Virgin to St. Germaine Cousin, a shepherdess, the
mistress observed, "The Blessed Virgin acts
that way with shepherdesses, doesn't she, Sister Marie-Bernard?" "Yes, my dear Mother,"
was all Bernadette said. More pointedly the day
Bernadette won a statue of St. Germaine Cousin
in a raffle, the mistress let fly a little barb: "A
shepherdess could not but fall into the hands of
another shepherdess!" That sarcasm got only
silence for an answer.

Far from hiding her deficiencies, she freely
revealed them, as on the day that Sister Isabelle
de Laverchère gave her a verb to conjugate as
an exercise. Instead of privately telling sister,
she said, in front of the whole class, "My dear
Sister, I can't do a verb." And to the same sister,
impatient at her lack of progress in reading,
who told her, "Sister Marie-Bernard, you'll
never learn to read!" her smiling answer was,

"Thank you, my dear Sister." Without any human respect she would ask her sisters to correct her letters before they were sent, because she knew they needed correction.

She did not want to be different but wanted so badly to be ordinary. When Bishop Forcade asked her if she had seen the Blessed Virgin again after the apparitions, or whether she had received any other extraordinary graces since then, her reply was, "Never. At present I'm like everyone else." She wanted to be "like everyone else," but everyone else would not let her; she was special. When the Sister Zelator took sick, the sisters wanted Bernadette to take over her duty of giving short, inspirational talks, with the hope that she would speak to them of the Blessed Virgin. Her answer was, "Oh! I couldn't say anything. I can't speak. I'm a stone. What can you expect from a stone?" When the novices gave her too much attention she told them she would leave their recreation if they did not treat her more normally and would have left, reports Sister Clémence Chasan, had the novices not agreed. One sister, Sister Henri Marsan, worshiped her nurse, Bernadette, and could not take her eyes off her. Noticing this, Bernadette said to her, "Don't look at me like that," and put her hand over Sister Henri's eyes. The result of that was, "I was so happy that she touched me that I kept my eyes closed a long while to keep the impressions of her fingers there." Sister Vincent Garros asked her one day what she was embroidering. "Oh! They'll make an alb of it to keep in the community," she said. "They regard me as something I am not." To Sister Eléonore Bonnet, who marveled at her fine embroidery, she said, "Anyone else could have done as much." Sister Gonzaga Champy asked her for a picture for another sister. "Yeş," said Bernadette, "but don't you want one for yourself?" "I wouldn't have dared to ask you for one," said sister. "That's not very nice," said Bernadette, "you must treat me more simply."

Her friend, Sister Marcelline Lannessans, wanted to learn how to make a good confession and asked Bernadette to go first and to speak a bit loud, not to hear her sins, but to see how she did it. Teasingly Bernadette answered her, "My dear friend, all honor to the great; you are my senior, so you must go first!"

She got a laugh out of knowing her picture was being sold in Lourdes for ten centimes. "That's all I'm worth" and "That's not much to be proud of," were her comments. When Sister Louise Brusson one day saw her cleaning toilets, she let her know it was far below her dignity to be doing such abject work. "It's my job and I'll do it the best I can," she answered her. She could turn the tables on a joker too. Sister Chantal Guinet told her one day, "Sister Marie-Bernard, you'll never be canonized!" "Why?" asked Bernadette. "Because you use snuff. St. Vincent de Paul almost missed being canonized because of his snuff box." "And you, Sister Chantal, who don't use snuff, you no doubt will be canonized!" was her retort.

The Cathedral of Nevers in January, 1874, had two new stain glass windows, portraying Bernadette: one of the apparitions and the other of Bernadette receiving her veil from Bishop Forcade. The Mother General had strongly objected to the bishop, but the bishop overruled her. The sisters attended solemn services at the cathedral, and, of course, were very curious about seeing the windows as well as knowing Bernadette's reaction, because she too had seen the windows. To Sister Antoinette Noirot, she said, "They made me very homely. Nothing to be vain about."

She usually saw through people wanting to see her, even to the bishop himself. "It's funny that a bishop would take time out to come to hear the sick sister's confessions, isn't it?" she commented on the unusual practice. Sister Victoire Girard, visiting the convent, asked the sister next to her to point out Bernadette. The sister said she would and disappeared. The following day she asked another sister the same thing, who said to her, "Why! You were next to her last night!" Sometimes she was not aware of what was happening, as Sister Julienne Capmartin gives an instance: Bishop Dreux-Brézé of Moulin knew Bernadette but wanted to see her again without her knowing it. Sister M...nie called Sister Julienne and told her to get Bernadette to bring napkins to her but then added, "You will go with her and when you reach the parlor windows, keep her there so that the Bishop of Moulin can see her without being seen." "That won't be easy," said Sister

Julienne, "because Bernadette won't allow the breaking of silence except for a good cause. She'll treat me as a blabber." "Let her," said Sister Mélanie. "Just stop her there on some pretext for a while." Sister Julienne got her to follow her, and at the right spot began to rave about a pretty, little flower growing there. "Isn't God good to create such a pretty flower! The prettiest in the whole garden..." all this while Bernadette faced the parlor windows. Sister Julienne continues, "I expected a reprimand, but no, she stopped, looked at the little flower, bent over and caressed it. Then thinking my discourse much too long, she began to walk toward the linen-room, with just one word for me, "Clacker!"

What she advised others she practiced herself. To Sister Madeleine Bounaix: "Don't put yourself first." And to Sister Vincent Garros: "Avoid talking about yourself. Don't try to stand out among the rest of the sisters." And to the same sister: "Don't wait for a compliment when you've done something worthwhile, otherwise you'll lose the merit of the good work."

"How lucky you are to remain in the mother house," her cousin, Sister Victoire Cassou, told her. "What would they have done with me? I'm good for nothing," she answered, although she admitted to others that she would have loved to do hospital work or to teach orphans. Her heart went out to orphans; in fact, Sister Eudoxia Bagnols used to ask for prayers for her orphans at Limoux. She agreed, with a proviso: "I'll pray for them but you pray for me, who am so proud." Sister Véronique Crillon complained to her one day that her classmate was a superior and she was not, adding, "You are the superior of the Infirmary." "Listen," said Bernadette, "I aspire to be superior only of myself, and I'm not doing too well at that!"

The long hours she spent sick were not idle. Scratching colored eggs with a penknife to produce various designs was tedious work, and Sister Casimir Callery, helping her, whined about the monotony. "What difference does it make to earn heaven scratching eggs or doing something else?" she answered her. And of the saints, she told her, "I would like writers to tell the defects of the saints in their lives, so that we could see how they corrected themselves." Finding her in the tribune, next to the infirmary, Sister Casimir asked her what she was doing there. Her answer, "I'm putting myself in a niche during my life, for fear of not being in one after I die!"

For a time she was not able to attend the community exercises and bemoaned her lot. A sister, noticing the cane she was using, said to her, "You have in your hand a most eloquent preacher!" "Yes," she answered smilingly, "they taught me to recall St. Ignatius' words: 'A religious should be in the hands of God and of her superiors like a stick,' but I find that it is not always easy and it costs me a lot." It humiliated her to have to be carried to the chapel for Mass and she worried about the sisters who carried her. They laughed at her and told her they could carry four like her. Her short stature and petite figure was also good for a laugh. Standing between two of the tallest sisters one day, she playfully said, "Look! Can't I think I'm something with my height!"

At the same time as she practiced humility, she could gently slip in a lesson on show. Sister Justine Vergeade, a postulant, had polished the copper balls on the bed posts in the infirmary to shiny perfection and boasted of it to Bernadette. "Yes, they sparkle," she answered. "You polished them brightly. You put your all in that because it shows." The lesson was not lost on Sister Justine.

She still received visitors at the close of her life, even though she was bedridden, with many physical pains and almost at the end of her patience. One of these, a visiting sister from another convent, tested her sorely by asking her to pray for a litany of causes, with a precise enumeration of each item of the litany. Though it was torture to have to listen, Bernadette showed all the patience in the world during this visit, but could not help herself when the sister finally left. "I'd rather see her heels than the tip of her nose," she said to her cousin Sister Victoire Cassou. "When one is suffering, one wants to be alone." "You'll say the same thing about me when I am gone," said her cousin. "Oh, no! my dear friend, it's not the same thing at all!"

To those sisters who stayed with her during the night, she begged pardon for all the complaining she did, which was only moans that escaped against her will. She wanted sisters who could sleep to stay by her side, and told them she would call them if she needed them.

Humble to the very end, she was heard to say, "I'm afraid! I have received so many graces and have profited so little from them!"

Teacher

Bernadette was hardly aware of the lessons she taught by just being her normal self. She could tell stories on herself to cheer up the postulants and novices and make them forget their petty troubles. Sister Claire Bordes retells two of these.

An old, sick sister asked Bernadette for some hot water, at which Bernadette left for the kitchen to ask Sister Cécile for some. When she got there she could not find Sister Cécile, so she drew the water from the faucet and was about to leave when Sister Cécile swooped down on her. "What are you doing here?" she asked. "I came to get hot water for a sick sister," Bernadette answered. "Ah! That's it! You have to ask permission for that. Put that water back where you got it!" scolded the sister. "But, my dear Sister, it comes from the faucet!" said Bernadette. Just then one of the Assistant Mothers, Mother Louise Férrand, came along and asked what was going on. "This little Sister has come to take water without permission," said Sister Cécile. Mother Louise settled things by tapping Bernadette on the shoulder and telling her, "Take the water to your patient." Bernadette left, laughing at the thought of putting the water back up the faucet, but Sister Cécile caught her laughing and said to Mother Louise, "Look at that little bit of a Sister. She's laughing. A bigger Sister would have left sniveling!"

Bernadette had a second run-in with Sister Cécile. Caring for the same sick sister, she went to the kitchen to get matches, but the bell rang for a community exercise. "What time is it, Sister?" asked Sister Cécile. "4:05." "What time are novices supposed to come to get matches?" "3.30." "Next time you come when you're supposed to...." Bernadette took the box of matches and started out but was stopped short by Sister Cécile. "And what of the others? What will they have if you take all the matches? Take what you need and put the box back where it belongs!"

Then there was the incident of the cornette. The sister in charge of mending gave her a ragged cornette to repair. She took it to the infirmary and told Sister Martha, "I'll never finish mending this!" "Don't bother your head about it," said Sister Martha, "I have some we use to swab up with that are not as bad as that. I'll give you one." Bernadette took the one Sister gave her and mended that one and brought it back to the sister in charge of mending. "This isn't the one I gave you," she said. "No," said Bernadette, "Sister Martha changed that one for a better one." This incident was reported to the mistress of novices, who gave Bernadette a good scolding. When Sister Madeleine Bounaix, to whom she was telling the story, tried to sympathize with her, she would not hear of it.

"Sister was right," Bernadette said, "the cornette was not the one she gave me."

She told Father Sempé, the director of the grotto-priests, when he came to visit her, how her vanity was punished when she was a child. Her uncle, Aunt Bernarde's husband, brought home a number of rings from a trip he had taken, but though they fit the fingers of the other little girls, they were all too big for her little fingers. To console her, her uncle promised he would get her one that fit. When he did bring one, it was too small; but Bernadette, by using all of her strength and her teeth, forced the ring on. It was not too long before the finger began to swell and pain terribly. The ring had to be sawed off with a small file. Laughing heartily, she told Father Sempé, "I never again wanted a ring!"

She could also teach by sermonettes. Her friend from Lourdes, Sister Vincent Garros, must have also been her greatest despair. Sister Vincent tells this on herself: "When I got to the novitiate, I wasn't used to rising at 5:00. One morning in the chapel I fell asleep and landed on the floor. The infirmarians, Bernadette among them, rushed to me and carried me out of the chapel. They gave me a tonic, which I drank with relish, but I didn't tell them why I fell. I later told Sister Marie-Bernard, who lectured me on the abuse of the kindness of the infirmarians and on my sinning against humility. She was right. It was pride that prevented me from explaining my fall."

The same Sister Vincent forgot to replenish the mistress of novices' holy water font. To avoid being humiliated she put spittle on her fingers and smeared the inside of the font and offered the mistress some to bless herself. Bernadette got wind of this and told Sister Vincent that she lacked respect to a superior and to a sacred object. Sister answered, "I didn't want to lack respect, I just wanted to avoid being embarrassed." But Bernadette said, "You would have been made to kiss the floor! Big deal! Now you have to confess that and tell Mother Mistress." "All right, I'll confess it, but I surely won't tell Mother Mistress! Oh, no!" But in the end she did both.

In a highly religious atmosphere, it was easy for Bernadette to teach her fellows by dropping inspirational gems for them to ponder and, of course, she felt not the slightest bit of embarrassment in so doing. Some of the sisters remembered these years afterwards.

Sister Emilienne Duboé remembers her telling her, "If we had faith, we'd see God in everything," not an original saying, but one Sister Emilienne remembered because Bernadette said it.

She who had received so many favors through the use of her eyes could not help having a good laugh with Sister Emilie Marcillac, at a novice who went around with her eyes closed. "Look at Sister," said Bernadette, "if she didn't have her companion to lead her, she would have had an accident. Why close your eyes when it is so necessary to have them open!"

Sick in the infirmary with Bernadette, Sister Victoire Talbotier said to her about the meals served there, "Sister Marie-Bernard, how you accept whatever they bring you!" Bernadette answered her, "God sends it to me; how can I refuse it?" Certain foods did not agree with her, but she never complained about them, noticed Sister Emilie Marcillac. This sister brought her such a meal one day and heard Bernadette say with a sweet smile, "It's my penance you're bringing me." And speaking of meals, Sister Emilie recalled the day she had a postulant helping her carry the meals to the sick sisters. The poor postulant dropped her end of the board and the whole mess fell to the floor. Petrified, Sister Emilie cried out, "We're lost! We're lost!" Hearing all the commotion, Bernadette came to help them. "Be quiet! you're not lost," said Bernadette, "I'll fix it up with Sister Martha." True to her word, she did fix it up with the Sister Infirmarian. Meeting Sister Emilie the following day, she said to her, "You're not lost after all!"

She could never hold anything against anyone who hurt her. Sister Joseph Caldairou repeats what she heard her say, "Oh! I pardon them with all my heart." Or her more usual answer when someone reminded her of some pain caused by others, "I don't remember that." She made it a point not to remember injuries.

Sister Stanislaus Tourriol tells this: One day one of the teachers in the novitiate, trying to impress them with the idea of promptitude in answering the bell, told them of the religious to whom the Child Jesus appeared at the same time the bell rang for a community exercise. The religious left the Child Jesus and answered the bell. "Oh!" said Bernadette, "I would have gone to the exercise, all right; but I would have taken the Child Jesus along with me!"

Sister Emilienne Robert complained to Bernadette one day about the difficulties of self-correction. "How can you say that?" asked Bernadette. "Having received the bread of the strong so often, how can you have so little courage?" And to a discouraged Sister Hélène Sutra, who told her, "It's easy for you to be patient and resigned, after all the favors and graces you received from the Blessed Virgin!" she answered, "That is true. I have been spoiled and very privileged; but then if I didn't correspond to such favors, what an ingrate I would be and how guilty!"

The Mother General, leaving for Paris, asked the sisters for their requests. Seeing Bernadette in the group, she asked her if she wanted anything. Spontaneously, Bernadette exclaimed, "Oh! Bring me back the love of God!"

She inspired all the sisters without ever intending to, as on the day her class took the habit. Sister Charles Ramillon and she promised to say an "Ave Maria" for each other for perseverance. After donning their new habits, they both came back and each said her "Ave" for the other. Sister Charles' prayer began, "My good Mother, I'm saying my 'Ave' only because

I promised to, since you have already assured her of her salvation; but, please, answer the prayer Sister Marie-Bernard is saying for me!"

The sisters, like the lay people, wanted Bernadette to touch their rosaries, but if she suspected this, she would not do it. Trickery had to be resorted to, to have her take their beads in her hands. "Look!" said Sister Stanislaus Bassignan, with the intention of passing her beads to Bernadette, "my rosary beads are rusty!" Bernadette's pedagogics left nothing wanting, "My dear friend," she said, "they're rusty because you don't say them often enough!"

Since Bernadette was being watched by everyone in the convent, there was very little she ever did that escaped notice; what one did not see, another did. They all admired her for her deep recollection in prayer; for her obedience to the rule; for her spirit of silence during times of silence; for her charity to others; for her low opinion of herself; for her lack of complaint; for her courage in physical suffering. She made the other sisters better sisters just by being among them.

Even when she did unusual things, the ending always had a typical Bernadette ending. On going to St. Joseph's Chapel on the convent grounds (where Bernadette was to be buried for forty-six years) to pay their daily visit, Bernadette noticed high on a vine a bunch of grapes that had been overlooked by the pickers. "What a pity to lose such a beautiful bunch of grapes," said Bernadette. "If we tried, we could get them." No sooner said than attempted. Sister

Saint-Michael Graffeuil, Sister Bernard Dalias, Sister Marguerite-Marie Magnie (who tells this story) and a fourth sister crossed their wrists to make a cradle. Off came Bernadette's shoes and up in the cradle she hopped; and all four-feet-seven-inches of her was hoisted up to retrieve the forgotten grapes. The typical Bernadette ending is that once she had the grapes, she ran to the mistress of novices up ahead on the path to ask permission for the sisters to enjoy the grapes they saved.

Mother Vauzous, the mistress of novices, could not keep up a steady cold treatment of Bernadette day in and day out. The mistress was attracted to Bernadette and exhibited her confidence in Bernadette by often sending her homesick and troubled postulants and novices; by allowing her, a professed sister, to fraternize with the postulants and novices during their recreations; by naming her to "Tell the Hour," reminding all the sisters present to renew the good intentions of their morning offering. Even at times going so far as to clearing her throat in passing by the infirmary door when Bernadette was sick in bed, to let her know that she was thinking of her in her suffering. "I couldn't answer her signal last night, because it was a time of silence," said Bernadette to Sister Joseph Durand.

Miseries

What the Mother General had said on Bernadette's profession day turned out all too true. "Since she is sick most of the time, we will give her something to do in the infirmary, that will be just the thing." All the time she spent as a nun was an up and down existence; up for a while and down for much of the time.

Her asthma attacks, which she had experienced since she was six, she was beginning to cope with a little better. Attacks came and went, some so bad that everyone thought that she would never get through them, for hardly being able to breathe; but then there were remissions that left her relatively healthy. Had it been asthma alone that affected her, her life would have been more or less bearable, but tuberculosis began to take its toll. Bouts of coughing would leave her weak; spitting up blood got so bad that the convent doctor thought that one of these spells would finish her. Because her stomach had been ruined in her childhood, the convent fare gave her digestive system a difficult time. Her bones and teeth began to decay as time went by, and towards the end of her life a tubercular tumor on her right knee caused intolerable pain. She used a cane, then crutches for a time, but at last she had to be carried to chapel and to the parlor, because she lost the use of her legs. Finally, she could not leave her bed at all. Sister Alphonse Guerre, tending her in her last days, said that her body was one big sore. To turn her over, so as to give her a little relief, was pure agony. The sister and she would try to perform the maneuver in unison; but as careful as they tried to be, the pain was excruciating.

Almost till the very end, she continued to try to cheer up her attendants and the sisters who came to visit her. She tried so hard not to disturb her night-nurses and would apologize to them for her twistings and turnings during the nights, all of which seemed to be interminable. She would tell them to sleep, and, if she needed them, she would call them. She dismissed one sister because that sister could not catnap during her vigil, too much worried about Bernadette's comfort.

Added to all her bodily ills were her mental troubles. The further away the apparitions drifted, the less her memory could recall the details. This frightened her to the point that she once said, "What if I had been mistaken?"

To make matters still worse for Bernadette, a Jesuit historian, Father Leonard Cros, got permission to write the history of the apparitions. He had interviewed many of the witnesses but wanted most desperately to interview the main witness, Bernadette. The superiors objected because of Bernadette's poor health, but that did not dissuade the historian with his scent for the truth. Armed with a brief from Pope Leo XIII, he descended on Bernadette with the zeal of a Grand Inquisitor. His methods were harsh and aggressive, and this terrified Bernadette, who not only became more forgetful but more confused. The ordeal was exhausting, and since most of the questions were mostly of the minute details of the visions, things her memory had lost, this shattered her peace of mind. Her superiors vehemently opposed this torture, but the only relief they were able to get was to stop Father Cros' personal visits, by having him submit his questions in writing, with Father Sempé, the director of the Grotto-Fathers, posing them and writing down her answers. This last investigation most probably hastened her death.

During these trying times, her soul was being wrung with thoughts, bordering on despair. Had she done enough to show her gratitude for all the favors she had received? Would she be punished for not corresponding to such privileges?

Her sufferings reached their peak during Easter Week, 1879. Up to now she had never sought relief, but had accepted all the pain that came along. Her endurance was coming to the breaking point. To Sister Cécile Pogès, in charge of the convent pharmacy, she pleaded, "If you could only find some drug...anything... to pick me up. I'm so weak I can't breathe.... Send me some strong vinegar to sniff."

She sensed her end coming and rid herself of her last possessions; she gave away the holy pictures she had hanging on the drapes of her bed and kept only a crucifix. "This is enough for me," she said.

On Easter Day a constant cough racked her tiny frame. To Sister Saint-Cyr Jollet and a group of sisters who came to visit her, she said, "This morning after communion I asked our Lord for a five-minute respite to be able to talk to Him in comfort, but He would not give it to me.... My passion will last till my death."

On Easter Monday she said her last goodbye to her dear friend, Sister Bernard Dalias, visiting the motherhouse, "Adieu...Bernard...this time it's the end." And remembering the millstones of her childhood, she said to Sister Léontine Villaret, "I am ground like a grain of wheat."

On Easter Tuesday she went to communion, but during the morning asked to go back to confession, worried about her salvation. After hearing her confession, the chaplain, Father Febvre, gave her the Plenary Indulgence at the Hour of Death. He told her to renew with love the sacrifice of her life, to which, with a surprisingly strong voice, she answered, "What sacrifice? It's not a sacrifice to quit a life in which it is so difficult to belong to God!" In the evening, Mother Nathalie Portat, in whom Bernadette had always had much confidence, came to see her. "My dear Sister," she told her, "I'm afraid. I received so many graces and I profited so little from them!" Mother Nathalie's consoling words struck the right chord, for at the end of her encouragement, Bernadette seemed to be relieved of a great burden and said, "Ah! Thank you so much!" Sister Alphonse Guerre, who nursed her on her last night on earth, testifies that it was a night of interminable suffering.

At 11:30 Easter Wednesday morning, she could no longer stand being in bed and asked to be moved to an armchair. At 12:30 p.m., Mother Marie-Josephine Forestier, assisting her, thought her so far gone that she had the community alerted. The chaplain, Father Febvre, was sent for and found her gasping for breath. She again went to confession and then weakly repeated the prayers suggested to her. She took her crucifix and pressed it to her heart, but she was so feeble that a sister attached her crucifix to her robe, so that it would stay fixed. About 2:00, Mother Eleonore Cassagnes said to her, "You are on the cross." She extended her arms towards a hanging crucifix and said, "My Jesus! Oh! How I love You!"

At 2:15 one of her companions said to her, "Sister, you are suffering much...." "It's all good for heaven," she answered. "I'll ask our Immaculate Mother to give you consolation," said the sister. "No!" said Bernadette, "not consolation, but strength and patience!" She then remembered the special blessing at the hour of death Pope Pius IX had given her and asked for the letter but she was told it was only necessary to make her intention and invoke the name of

Jesus. "My God, I love You with all my heart, with all my soul and with all my strength," she prayed. At 2:55 the convent bell rang for the community to say their daily litany. Since Bernadette seemed to want to rest, the chaplain left and the sisters returned to the chapel, leaving only the infirmarians with her.

At 3:00 she was seized with pain, and the sister infirmarian sprinkled her with holy water. She took her crucifix and kissed the sacred wounds. Mother Nathalie entered and seeing her, Bernadette said, "My dear Sister, forgive.... Pray for me.... Pray for me!" Mother Nathalie and the infirmarians knelt and prayed. Extending her arms in the form of a cross, Bernadette cried out, "My God!" and then joined in the "Hail Mary" with the kneeling sisters. "Holy Mary, Mother of God..." and repeated twice, "pray for me, poor sinner." She then made a sign for something to drink, but before sipping a few drops, made her usual beautiful sign of the cross, learned from her Lady at the grotto, so long ago. She took the offered drink, inclined her head and died, supporting herself on the arm of Sister Gabrielle Vigouroux, who had replaced her as infirmarian six years before. It was April 16, 1879; Bernadette was thirty-five years old.

No more would she have to gasp for breath; no more would she have to drag herself around, supported on a painful right knee; no more would she have to cough her nights away; no more aches and pains. Neither would she be exposed any more to the unending line of visitors, wanting to question her, over and over, about her visions; nor would she have to submit again to the humiliations of her superiors, reserved solely for her; nor would she have to undergo the daily scrutiny of her fellow-sisters, expecting so much of her. All her troubles, physical and mental, were over. She was with God.

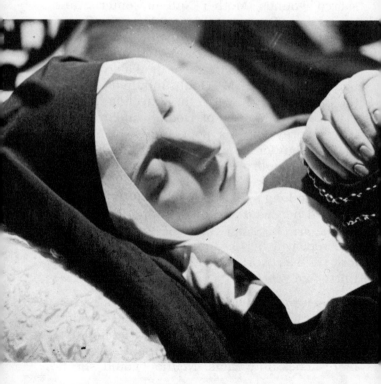

Epilogue

As soon as the news of Bernadette's death leaked out from the convent walls, people streamed in droves to the convent to pay their last respects. They had called her a saint since she was fourteen; now they knew she was one. They had pestered her without let-up in life; they could not now leave her alone in death.

It was not the custom of the Sisters of Nevers to embalm their deceased members; neither did they have Bernadette's body embalmed. They changed their rules in one regard: her burial place. They buried their nuns in the local cemetery, but they made an exception for Bernadette. They asked the authorities for permission to bury her in St. Joseph's Chapel on the convent grounds, a chapel that in the past Bernadette had so often visited. Her oaken coffin with a lead lining was finally buried May 30th. All the intervening time since her death was taken up by the usual red tape needed for the unusual burial place.

Her funeral Mass had been delayed because of the crowds, but, in spite of that, her body was as relaxed as though she were sleeping. This so impressed the archpriest of the Cathedral that he called in the Superintendent of Police to be a witness to the fact and to attest to the unusual appearance of the body.

So many people visited her grave in the years that followed—many of whom received their requests—that on August 20, 1908, an ecclesiastical court began its first inquiry into the life and miracles of Bernadette. One-hundred-and-thirty-two more sessions followed. As part of the investigation, a legal and canonical identification of the body had to be made, as well as authenticating its condition. On September 22, 1909, Church and civil authorities attended the ceremony. A table, covered with a white cloth, was prepared to receive what was left of Bernadette's body. The coffin lid was removed and the lead lining cut away, only to reveal her perfectly preserved body, emitting not the slightest offensive odor. The habit she had been buried in was moist, the cross she held was covered with verdigris, and the rosary intertwining her fingers, rusted. Though the examiners did not want to speak of a miracle, because, given the right circumstances, bodies sometimes become mummified and last a long time. In Bernadette's case, however, what with all her sicknesses and the condition of her body the day she died, and what with the humidity of the burial place in St. Joseph's Chapel, it was impossible not to be amazed at the preservation of her body after being thirty years in the ground. The sisters washed the body, put a new habit on it, placed it in a new coffin, double lined with zinc covered with silk, and it was reburied in St. Joseph's Chapel.

Relying on the decisions of the Congregation of Rites, which had received all the documents of the inquiry, Pope Pius X signed the decree for the introduction of Bernadette's cause for beatification, August 13, 1913. Bernadette had a new title, "Venerable."

Because of World War I there was a delay in the opening of the new investigation. It finally began September 17, 1917 and included two-hundred-and-three sessions. This Commission had Bernadette's body re-exhumed on April 3, 1919, and, as at the first exhumation ten years previously, they again found the body intact. It was placed in a new coffin and reburied in St. Joseph's Chapel. All the documents of this Commission were turned over to the Congregation of Rites February 20, 1920.

For the final identification of the body, previous to her beatification, it was exhumed for the last time April 18, 1925. Relics, which were to be sent to Rome, Lourdes and the houses of the Sisters of Nevers, were removed by Doctor Comte, a surgeon. After this the body was entirely swathed in bandages, except for the face and hands. Because it was feared that the darkened tinge to the face and the shrunken eyes and nose would make an unpleasant impression on the public, a precise imprint of the face was molded so that the firm of Pierre Imans of Paris could make a light wax mask, based on the mold and on genuine photos. Imprints of the hands were also taken for the same reason. The body was then placed in the Chapel of Saint Helen in the convent of Nevers, and the doors of the chapel were closed and sealed so that no one could get in.

Pope Pius XI declared Bernadette "Blessed," on June 14, 1925.

When the gilded bronze and transparent crystal shrine arrived from the firm of Armand Caillat of Lyons, the sisters dressed the body in a new habit; and the sculptor took the light wax masks, made from the molds taken in April, and placed them on the face and hands. The body was then put in its hermetically-sealed shrine August 3, 1925, and placed in the main chapel of the convent of Nevers, where it has remained on view ever since. To the wonder of all viewers, after so many years, one hundred in 1979, she seems peacefully asleep.

Now it was only a matter of examining and authenticating two new miracles, attributed to Bernadette's intercession, to have her sainted. In the course of the next few years this was done, and fittingly, on the feast of the Immaculate Conception, December 8, 1933, Bernadette was canonized by Pope Pius XI. Her saint's day is February 18, the day her Lady made the promise of making her happy forever in the next world.

What of the Lady's grotto? More than one-hundred-and-twenty years have gone since the apparitions at Lourdes. That sleepy, little town awoke in 1858 and grew from a population of 4,000 to about 20,000 today. Pilgrims keep coming to the grotto; in recent years in numbers of above two million (four million and a half in 1978), many of them making the processions Bernadette's Lady requested. Besides the original crypt, three basilicas and spacious chapels have been built to accommodate the multitudes. The little spring Bernadette scratched into existence now produces 27,000 gallons a day. Countless "miracles" have been claimed by people using the water, and doctors of all faiths continue to test the cures. Actually, only sixty-four cures have been declared miracles by the Church, as of 1978. This miraculous water has been piped to baths, where the sick bathe or are bathed; and healthy people may do the same if they wish. Some of the water from the spring is reserved, put into containers and shipped all over the world to help alleviate the miseries of believers.

The secret of Lourdes is belief. There are still those who won't believe any of the events of the grotto ever took place; but with so many tangible proofs so easy to verify, they have trouble trying to justify their disbelief. Believers cannot express their joy and gratitude for the kindness of the Lady to the girl she so highly favored and for the results of her graciousness. They are also extremely elated that the Lady and the girl, Bernadette, are now inseparably united.

Highlights of Bernadette's Life

1844	Jan. 7	Born
	Jan. 9	Baptized
	Nov.	Taken to Bartres to foster-mother
1845	Feb. 13	Jean, a brother, born (dies in 3 months)
	Oct.	Brought back to Lourdes
1846	Oct. 19	Marie "Toinette," a sister, born
1848	Dec. 10	Jean-Marie, a brother, born (dies 2 yrs. later)
1851	May 13	Another Jean-Marie, a brother, born
1854	mid-summer	Family turned out of Boly Mill and moves to Laborde's House, to Arcizac-les-Anglès, to Rives-Soubies' House in the next two years
1855	Feb. 28	Justin, a brother, born Cholera epidemic—Bernadette affected but recovers. Is employed at her Aunt Bernarde's bar at the corner of Bourg and Baous Streets
1856	May	Family moves to "The Cachot"
1857	end of June	Goes to Bartrès—shepherdess

1858	c. Jan. 21	Returns to Lourdes—enrolls in catechism class
	Feb. 11	1st apparition
	Feb. 14	2nd apparition
	Feb. 18	3rd apparition
	Feb. 19	4th apparition
	Feb. 20	5th apparition
	Feb. 21	6th apparition
	Feb. 23	7th apparition
	Feb. 24	8th apparition
	Feb. 25	9th apparition
	Feb. 27	10th apparition
	Feb. 28	11th apparition
	March 1	12th apparition
	March 2	13th apparition
	March 3	14th apparition
	March 4	15th apparition
	March 25	16th apparition
	April 7	17th apparition
	June 3	Makes First Holy Communion
	July 16	18th apparition
	middle of Sept.	Family moves out of "The Cachot"
1859	Sept. 10	Bernard-Pierre, a brother, born—godchild
1860	Feb. 5	Receives Confirmation
	July 15	Moves into the Hospice of Lourdes
1862	end of March	In bed with pneumonia
	April 20	Goes to grotto—falls ill again
	April 28	Receives Extreme Unction

1863	Sept. 23	Bishop Forcade of Nevers visits Hospice
1864	Feb. 4	Another Jean, a brother, born (dies Sept. 11)
	April 4	Solemn inauguration of Fabisch's statue at grotto, but Bernadette is too ill to go.
		Decides to become a Sister of Nevers
	Oct. 4	Seven week vacation at Momères
1865	Feb. 12	Justin, a brother, dies at age ten
	end of year	Admitted as a postulant at the Hospice
1866	Jan. 9	A little sister born but dies at birth
	May 21	Present at the inauguration of the Crypt
	June 25	Last visit to Bartrès
	July 3	Last visit to the grotto
	July 4	Leaves Lourdes forever
	July 5	At Bordeaux
	July 6	At Périgueux
	July 7	Arrives at Nevers
	July 8	Tells assembled community of her visions
	July 29	Takes novice's habit—now Sister Marie-Bernard
	c. Aug. 15	Sick in infirmary
	Sept. 3	Abed in infirmary
	Oct. 25	Receives Extreme Unction second time
	Dec. 8	Her mother dies

1867	Feb. 2	Resumes life as a novice
	Oct. 30	Makes her religious profession.
		Receives her "destination" —the mother house
		Named Assistant-Infirmarian
1868	Feb. 4	Picture-taking session
1869	Oct. 13	Writes "Protestation" for Henri Lassèrre
	Nov. 16	Father Sempé visits for his defense
1870	April 12	Takes full duties of Infirmarian
		French Army converts convent into hospital
1871	March 4	Her father dies
1873	Jan.	Falls ill again
	June 3	Receives Extreme Unction for third time
	Nov. 5	Is relieved of full duties in infirmary
1874	Jan.	Appointed Assistant Infirmarian and Assistant Sacristan
1875	Nov.	Life as an invalid begins
1877	Sept. 8	Dean Peyramale dies
	Dec. 16	Writes letter to Pius IX
1878	Sept. 22	Takes perpetual vows
	Dec. 12	Interrogation by Fr. Sempé on visions
	Dec. 18	Visit from her brother Jean-Marie

	Dec. 31	Interrogation by Fr. Sempé on visions
1879	Jan. 22	Interrogation by Fr. Sempé on visions
	Feb. 19	Interrogation by Fr. Sempe on visions
	March 18	Toinette and her husband visit
	March 28	Receives Extreme Unction fourth time
	April 15	Very ill
	April 16	Dies at 35
1908	Aug. 20	1st Ecclesiastical Inquiry into life and miracles
1909	Sept. 22	1st exhumation
	Oct. 23	Congregation of Rites receives documents
1913	Aug. 13	Piux X signs decree for the introduction of cause for beatification
1917	Sept. 17	2nd Ecclesiastical Inquiry
1919	April 3	2nd exhumation
1920	Feb. 20	Congregation of Rites receives documents
1923	Nov. 18	Pius XI publishes decree on heroic nature of her virtues
1925	April 18	3rd exhumation
	June 14	Declared "Blessed" by Pius Xl
	Aug. 3	Preserved body placed in shrine
1933	Dec. 8	Canonized by Pius XI

Hail Holy Queen OS

Rev. John H. Collins, SJ

Moving reflections on this prayer to our Lady. Full-color illustrations. 80 pages

cloth $3.00; paper $2.00 — MA0040

Mary, Hope of the World

Rev. James Alberione, SSP, STD

A brilliant consideration of Mary under these aspects: in the mind of God, prophecies, and the longing of humanity; in her earthly life as Co-redemptrix of mankind; in her life of glory in heaven, in the Church and in the heart of the faithful. 222 pages

cloth $4.00; paper $3.00 — MA0060

Mary, Mother and Model

Rev. James Alberione, SSP, STD

The history and aim of 30 Marian feasts, their part in the Breviary, and the benefits to be derived from their observance. Illustrated. 237 pages

cloth $4.00; paper $3.00 — MA0070

Mary of Nazareth

Igino Giordani

In *Mary of Nazareth* we follow God's spotless Mother from the moment she received the Archangel's tremendous message at Nazareth, to the moment of her bodily passage into glory. Thereafter we follow her through history and see her grow in the love of men. Beautifully illustrated with three sections of Madonna art pieces by Panigati and Nagni. 182 pages

cloth $6.00; paper $5.00 — MA0080

Mary, Queen of Apostles

Rev. James Alberione, SSP, STD

On Mary's mission of giving Jesus to the world. Superb approach to the imitation of Mary in the apostolates of desires, prayer, example, suffering and action. 348 pages

cloth $4.00; paper $3.00 — MA0090

Mary "The Servant of the Lord"

M. Miguens, O.F.M.

An ecumenical effort is behind this scriptural approach to the Blessed Mother. The writer's purpose is to analyze the biblical statements about Mary and to place them in the appropriate scriptural setting. Mary is described in terms of all those "servants" of the Lord down the ages through whose agency God gradually and firmly carried out and continued His saving design. 198 pages

cloth $3.75; paper $2.25 — MA0095

Mary, Star of the Sea

Rev. Albert Barbieri, SSP

"St. Bernard's famous words concerning Mary, Star of the Sea, form the subject of these thirty-one lofty meditations on Marian instructions, illustrated by appropriate examples." Rev. Gabriel M. Roschini, OSM 250 pages

cloth $3.50; paper $2.50 — MA0100

Our Lady Among Us

Rev. Valentino Del Mazza, S.D.B.

Marian devotion grows through a deeper understanding of her role in salvation history. Her titles, her position in the Church, her privileges, virtues, glories and apostolates are the framework of this magnificent portrait of Mary who always lives among us.

169 pages

cloth $4.00; paper $3.00 — MA0110

Ten Series of Meditations on the Mysteries of the Rosary

Rev. John Ferraro

Practical reflections compiled into ten series, making it possible to meditate points during each Hail Mary. Renders the recitation of the rosary more profound and fruitful. 232 pages

cloth $3.50; paper $2.25 — MA0120

That Motherly Mother of Guadalupe

Rev. L.M. Dooley, SVD

Mary's graciousness in her dealings with Juan Diego, even today, after a lapse of 430 years, enraptures the reader's heart. "A handsome, beautifully illustrated and excellently written volume." "Prairie Messenger" 80 pages
cloth $2.25; paper $1.25 — MA0130

True Devotion to the Blessed Virgin

St. Louis Grignon de Montfort

St. Louis Grignon de Montfort wrote his work to clarify our Lady's place in our lives, her place in the Mystical Body. His style may be of his time, but his theology is timeless—and that is why Popes and theologians, generation after generation, have called "The True Devotion" a classic. 204 pages
cloth $3.00 — MA0140

Cove of Wonders

Rev. Alphonse M. Cappa, S.S.P.

The enticing story of Fatima is presented in a popular style, recalling the secrets confided to three young children by Mary, the Mother of God, and the wonders she has worked at that heavenly cove. 300 pages
cloth $4.50; paper $3.25 — MA0026

Please order from any of the following addresses.

Daughters of St. Paul

IN MASSACHUSETTS
 50 St. Paul's Ave. Jamaica Plain, Boston, MA 02130;
   617-522-8911; 617-522-0875;
 172 Tremont Street, Boston, MA 02111; **617-426-5464;**
   617-426-4230
IN NEW YORK
 78 Fort Place, Staten Island, NY 10301; **212-447-5071**
 59 East 43rd Street, New York, NY 10017; **212-986-7580**
 7 State Street, New York, NY 10004; **212-447-5071**
 625 East 187th Street, Bronx, NY 10458; **212-584-0440**
 525 Main Street, Buffalo, NY 14203; **716-847-6044**
IN NEW JERSEY
 Hudson Mall — Route 440 and Communipaw Ave.,
   Jersey City, NJ 07304; **201-433-7740**
IN CONNECTICUT
 202 Fairfield Ave., Bridgeport, CT 06604; **203-335-9913**
IN OHIO
 2105 Ontario St. (at Prospect Ave.), Cleveland, OH 44115; **216-621-9427**
 25 E. Eighth Street, Cincinnati, OH 45202; **513-721-4838**
IN PENNSYLVANIA
 1719 Chestnut Street, Philadelphia, PA 19103; **215-568-2638**
IN FLORIDA
 2700 Biscayne Blvd., Miami, FL 33137; **305-573-1618**
IN LOUISIANA
 4403 Veterans Memorial Blvd., Metairie, LA 70002; **504-887-7631;**
   504-887-0113
 1800 South Acadian Thruway, P.O. Box 2028, Baton Rouge, LA 70821
   504-343-4057; 504-343-3814
IN MISSOURI
 1001 Pine Street (at North 10th), St. Louis, MO 63101; **314-621-0346;**
   314-231-1034
IN ILLINOIS
 172 North Michigan Ave., Chicago, IL 60601; **312-346-4228**
IN TEXAS
 114 Main Plaza, San Antonio, TX 78205; **512-224-8101**
IN CALIFORNIA
 1570 Fifth Avenue, San Diego, CA 92101; **714-232-1442**
 46 Geary Street, San Francisco, CA 94108; **415-781-5180**
IN HAWAII
 1143 Bishop Street, Honolulu, HI 96813; **808-521-2731**
IN ALASKA
 750 West 5th Avenue, Anchorage AK 99501; **907-272-8183**
IN CANADA
 3022 Dufferin Street, Toronto 395, Ontario, Canada
IN ENGLAND
 128, Notting Hill Gate, London W11 3QG, England
 133 Corporation Street, Birmingham B4 6PH, England
 5A-7 Royal Exchange Square, Glasgow G1 3AH, England
 82 Bold Street, Liverpool L1 4HR, England
IN AUSTRALIA
 58 Abbotsford Rd., Homebush, N.S.W., Sydney 2140, Australia